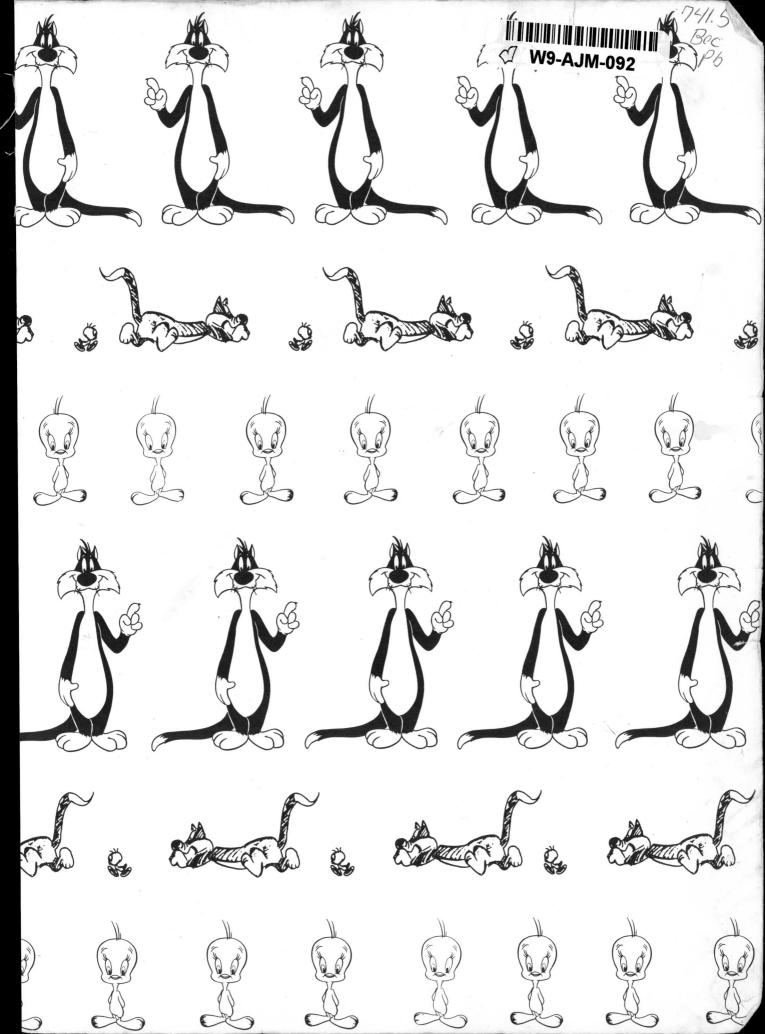

W9-AJM-092

741.5
Bec
Pb

WITHDRAWN

THE CLAREDON KITTE.

"I TAWT I TAW A PUDDY TAT"

FIFTY YEARS OF SYLVESTER AND TWEETY

BY JERRY BECK
with Shalom Auslander

Henry Holt and Company
New York

103250

EAU CLAIRE DISTRICT LIBRARY

B+T 11/4/94 #19.95

Page 1: *Storyboard sketch by Rod Scribner from "Birdy and the Beast" (1944).* *Pages 2-3:* *Publicity cel.* *Below:* *Publicity sketch, early 1950s.* *Opposite:* *Sylvester rests during a break on "The Bugs Bunny Show" (1960).*

All characters depicted are © Warner Bros. Inc.

LOONEY TUNES, all character names, and related slogans are Trademarks of Warner Bros., Inc.

Henry Holt books are available at special discounts for bulk purchases for sales promotions, premiums, fund-raising, or educational use. Special editions or book excerpts can also be created to specification.

For details contact:
Special Sales Director
Henry Holt and Company, Inc.
115 West 18th Street
New York, New York 10011

First American Edition—1991

Printed in Hong Kong
Recognizing the importance of preserving the written word, Henry Holt and Company, Inc., by policy, prints all of its first editions on acid-free paper. ∞

10 9 8 7 6 5 4 3 2 1

Copyright © 1991 by Sammis Publishing Corp.

All rights reserved, including the right to reproduce this book or portions thereof in any form.

Published in the United States by Henry Holt and Company, Inc., 115 West 18th Street, New York, New York 10011.

Published in Canada by Fitzhenry & Whiteside Limited, 195 Allstate Parkway, Markham, Ontario L3R 4T8.

The following frame enlargements are © 1944 The Vitaphone Corp. Ren. 1971 United Artists Television Inc.: pages 31 center, 37, 38, 42, 44, 45, 49, 87, 88, 90, 91, 93, 94, 95.

Photography on the following pages by Ruth Clampett: 6-7, 34, 35, 36, 37, 38, 39, 40, 41, 42, 43, 45 bottom, 48, 66 top, 86, 88, 89, 124, 127.

Prepared and produced by Layla Productions, Inc. and Sammis Publishing Company.
Designed by Alan Mogel.
Typesetting by WLCR Graphics.

Library of Congress Cataloging-in-Publication Data

Beck, Jerry.
   "I tawt I taw a puddy tat": Fifty years of Sylvester and Tweety/ Jerry Beck.—1st American ed.
      p.   cm.
   1. Tweety. (Fictitious character)   2. Sylvester (Fictitious character)   3. Warner Bros. Cartoons—History.   I. Title.
NC1766.UU52W37334   1991
741.5'09794'03—dc20   91-16428
ISBN 0-8050-1644-9   CIP

ACKNOWLEDGMENTS

We would like to thank the entire staff of Warner Bros. Classic Animation, especially Kathleen Helppie-Shipley, Lorri Bond, Charles Gaitz, and Darrell Van Citters and the staff of Warner/LCA, especially Karen McTier, Beverly Cannady, and Daniel Kletzky, for their cooperation and support of this project.

We would like to express our thanks to the heirs of Tweety's legacy: Bob Clampett, Jr., Ruth Clampett, Sody Clampett, and Robert McKimson, Jr. A special thank-you goes to Friz Freleng.

We would also like to acknowledge the following Tweety bird watchers who "taw a puddy tat" and contributed to this book: Mark Kausler, Dick May and Diana Brown of Turner Entertainment, Leonard Maltin, Steve Schneider, Mike and Jeanne Glad, Steve Ferzoco, Linda Simensky (who can be seen modeling her Tweety costume on page 68), Cheryl Chase, Nancy Johnson, Mike Kazaleh, Will Friedwald, Mike Barrier, Jim Korkis, John Cawley, The Shine Gallery, Chris and Len Surico, Stewart Ng and Leith Adams of the UCLA Warner Bros. Archive, Bill Strahan, Alison Juram, Eva Diaz, Barbara Miller, Mel Kaplan, Carmine Laietta, Lori Stein, Deena Stein, Michelle Stein, Raynard Stapleton, Samuel Jason, Shalom Auslander, Orli Ben-Tzion, David Pryor, Alex Lee, Anne Miller, the gang at Jellybean, Jay Hyams, Chani Yammer, Leslie Garisto, Eric Marshall, Alan Mogel, and John Sammis.

PHOTO CREDITS

We'd like to thank the following individuals and organizations for granting us permission to use illustrations from their collections:

Bob Clampett Collection © Bob Clampett Productions, Inc. All rights reserved, including the right to reproduce in any form): pp. 1, 5-6, 25 top right; 34 bottom; 35; 36; 38 top right; 39; 40-41; 43; 48; 53 top; 58; 63 left; 66 top; 68 top; 86; 89; 116; 124; 127; 143.

Steve Ferzoco: pp. 11; 78 bottom right; 80 right; 100 right.

Mike and Jeanne Glad: pp. 10 top; 26 left; 27 top left and right; 55; 60-61; 62 right; 95 bottom; 101 left; 114 left; 121; 126; 128 top and center; 129 bottom; 131; 141; 142 top; 154.

Leonard Maltin: pp. 16-17; 53 bottom.

Robert McKimson, Jr.: pp. 64; 79 bottom; 81 bottom 140 center.

Steve Schneider: 4; 12 right; 13; 14 right; 15; 18; 20-21; 24 right; 25 left; 27 top left and right; 32-33; 33 top; 44 bottom; 45 top right; 47; 52; 54; 58 top left; 63 right; 65 bottom; 66 center; 67 bottom left; 74 top; 75 top right; 76 left; 77 bottom; 78 bottom; 79 top; 81 top; 82; 83 bottom; 92 left; 97 bottom left; 98-99; 103 bottom; 109 bottom; 110 bottom; 115; 117 center left; 118-119; 120 right; 132-133; 138 top; 144 top; 152 right.

Warner Bros. Archive at the University of Southern California: pp. 26 top; 134 bottom; 140 top; 150, second.

We would also like to thank the **Animation Plus! Gallery** for the flip book on pages 87 to 159.

NOTE: The terms puddy tat and putty tat are used interchangeably throughout this book, as they were by the Warner artists. In Bob Clampett's cartoons, puttytat was used consistently; other directors and animators used whichever form they preferred. Warner Bros. has now endorsed the form "puddy tat."

CONTENTS

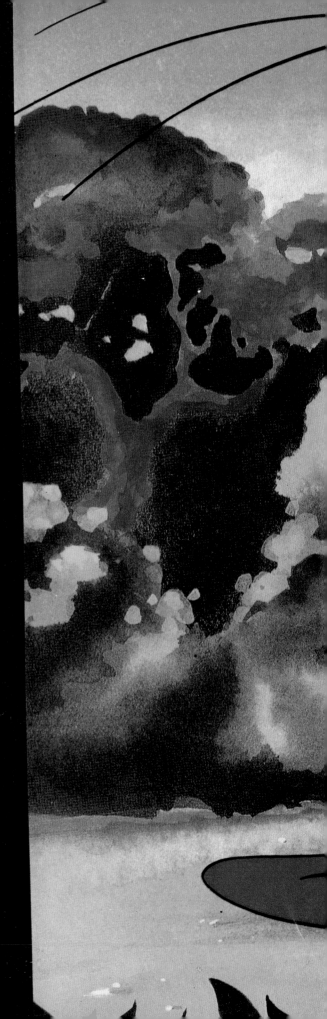

*Tweety heads for trouble in "Birdy
and the Beast" (1944) in a limited
edition cel from Bob Clampett
Animation Art.*

1
CAT AND CANARY

TWEETY

What could be more innocent than a lovable, peaceful baby canary? And what if that harmless little bird were stronger and smarter than the devious alley cat who stalks his every move? Therein lies the core of one of Warner Bros. most successful cartoon teams—the canary and cat known as Tweety and Sylvester.

Tweety was a timely canary. He appeared in the world of Warner Bros. cartoons in the 1940s, just when the Depression and World War II had shaken America out of its innocence. The Warner Bros. animators mirrored the new national attitude with smarter, tougher, and wiser characters (witness the hunted bunny rabbit with enough chutzpah to ask his hunter, "Eh, what's up, Doc?").

Tweety's life falls into two parts. He was created and directed in his first three film outings by Bob Clampett, Warners' king of the outrageous, who granted him a survival instinct that seemed almost cruel at times—in "Birdy and the Beast," Tweety puts out a fire in his enemy's mouth with a spritz of gasoline. Clampett left Warner Bros. in 1946, leaving Tweety in the capable hands of Friz Freleng, the master director who had been working with a clownish pussycat later named Sylvester; it was Freleng who teamed up the cat and canary. After that first pairing, nearly every Tweety cartoon—a total of fifty-six, including three that were nominated for and two that won Academy Awards—included Sylvester and was directed by Freleng.

The humor in Tweety's situation lies in the ability of this seemingly helpless bird to act so strongly and effectively in his own defense. No paranoid, Tweety doesn't imagine his foes, he really has them—and they actually want to *eat* him. The canary is never the instigator of his battles, but he never backs down from a fight. No one can blame him for his nonchalant aggression when it is carried out only in reaction to attack by enemies several times his size.

Tweety stays calm in the face of danger from Sylvester because he knows he is smarter. He can afford to be sympathetic—"Oh, the poor puddy tat, he

Previous pages: Model sheet poses of Tweety and Sylvester. **Below:** *Tweety tots up his victories in "Birdy and the Beast."*

The many faces of Tweety: innocent (top and opposite); angry in "Bad Ol' Puddy Tat" (1949, right); proud in "Tweet, Tweet, Tweety" (1951, far right)

fall down," Tweety often remarks—and even helpful—"Keep wowing, puddy tat, I'll save you," he calls to Sylvester, who is desperately rowing away from a waterfall, just as he seals his doom. Tweety's innocence doesn't get in the way of his eventual victory; he always comes up with a stick of dynamite, a pin to burst Sylvester's balloon, a blowtorch to destroy the contraptions Sylvester builds to catch him. More often than not, Tweety doesn't lay a toe on his adversary, for Sylvester's plans usually backfire on themselves. On the rare occasions when Tweety doesn't manage to protect himself, Granny or a helpful bulldog (whom Tweety awakes in the nick of time) is there to help. As Joe Adamson pointed out in *Bugs Bunny: Fifty Years and Only One Grey Hare*, Tweety, like Bugs Bunny and the Road Runner, is an "innocent"—"there is *no physical explanation* why their schemes should succeed and their adversary's consistently fail—that characters like Sylvester and Wile E. Coyote just can't get the hang of it. It may be an erratic, intractable Universe . . . but there will always be those who are in harmony with it."

When Tweety does retaliate, it's with a vengeance. Perhaps that is why Tweety is so popular. Who can't sympathize with the little guy who, when pushed

Below: Publicity and production artwork of the ever-confident Tweety. Opposite: Sylvester sets himself up for another fall in animation art by Virgil Ross from "A Mouse Divided" (1953).

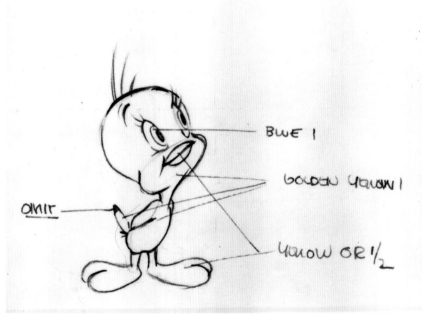

just too far, retaliates with his own wits (or his enemy's lack thereof)? When pushed, Tweety simply takes over, as he does in "Bad Ol' Puddy Tat": tricked into entering Sylvester's mouth he takes control of the cat's mind and body by playing an innocent game of choo-choo train, driving the cat like a runaway locomotive headfirst into a brick wall. Never mistake Tweety's innocence for ignorance; Tweety knows exactly what he's doing. In one of his earliest cartoons, he shows us his record of victories over puddy tats. He then reassumes his innocence and sadly shakes his head, commenting, "You know, I lose more puddy tats that way." We may sense a bit of gloating—but with Sylvester for a foe, can we blame him?

EAU CLAIRE DISTRICT LIBRARY

The many moods of Sylvester: stymied in "The Last Hungry Cat" (1961, top); shocked in "Who's Kitten Who" (1952, above); sinister (above right) and surprised (opposite) in production cels from the 1950s.

SYLVESTER

Porky Pig on Sylvester: "A yellow dog of a cowardly cat." Tweety on Sylvester: "A nasty ol' peeping tom cat."

Therein lies the general character of Sylvester (or Sylvester J. Pussycat, as he likes to style himself): the nasty-but-nice, fearsome-but-wimpy, clever-but-gullible cat who makes Tweety's life the exciting, never-ending chase it is. Or, as another bit player calls him, "You coward, you bully, you schmo."

Sylvester doesn't have just nine lives—he has about nine personalities as well. There's the Sylvester we see most often: the canary-chasing trouble-maker. This Sylvester fancies himself quite the genius. Each canary-catching scheme is more elaborate than the previous, but all seem to fail just as quickly. And with each successive failure, he becomes more frustrated, more determined, and, unfortunately for him, more injured. Tweety frustrates Sylvester into playing Tweety's game, a game of wits and ingenuity for which Sylvester is ill equipped. After a while, we wonder why Sylvester doesn't just give up. We get our answer in the Academy-Award winning "Birds Anonymous," when after trying to go "cold Tweety" and stop chasing birds, Sylvester is reduced to a blubbering idiot and sadly confesses, "I gotta have a bird! I'm weak, but I don't care! I can't help it! After all, I am a pussy cat."

Then there is the Sylvester who is a devoted father, teaching his curious son, Junior, how to catch a mouse. Even in this occupation he is outwitted. Junior must constantly show him the right way to catch a mouse or convince him to teach him how, even as Sylvester is in midst of another elaborate sure-to-fail plan. On more than one failed occasion Junior turns to the audience to ask, "I wonder if anyone would be interested in adopting a fatherless kitten?" In one of his encounters with Hippety Hopper, the kangaroo he forever mistakes for a giant mouse, Sylvester proudly states his condition with most of his prey: "I've got him right where he wants me."

In "Back Alley Oproar" we see an exuberant Sylvester, for once successful in his attempts to keep Elmer Fudd from getting a good night's sleep. Yet another Sylvester is the terrified traveling pet of Porky Pig (in Porky's words, "a crazy psychopathic cat"), while another is the devoted foe of Speedy Gonzales. Speedy has issued a standing threat: "Gringo Pussycat—eef I see you, I weel pool your tail out by eets root." The threat is carried out more than once.

All of these Sylvesters have one thing in common: the soul of a hungry alley cat who thinks he has it all figured out but succeeds only in outwitting himself. Rarely portrayed as a hero, Sylvester became the Warner Bros. all-around fall guy. Seeing Sylvester get it—being outrun by the fastest mouse in Mexico, being whacked by Granny's broomhandle, or being soundly beaten by a canary one-tenth his size—provides some of the funniest—if most painful—moments in cartoon history.

A SHARED DESTINY

The idea of a comedy team is not new, neither for human comedy nor for the animated kind. The teams of Tom and Jerry and Heckle and Jeckle are only the most obvious of the latter. The novelty of the Tweety-and- Sylvester team was that each of the two characters possessed his own distinct personality. These two characters were not created for the express purpose of supporting each other, as was the case with most other comedy teams (animated or otherwise), and they both led separate animation careers long before they ever even met. This novelty contributes to the mayhem and magic behind Tweety and Sylvester as a team.

In cartoon after cartoon, Tweety and Sylvester play out their combined destiny: forever will Sylvester yearn, and forever will Tweety turn him upside down and inside out. Sylvester grows in stature because of his determination; faced with a foe he can't outwit, we'd expect him to give up. But he doesn't. He comes back with one more scheme, one more device, one more sure-fire trap.

On the surface, the symbolism is rather simple. Tweety represents the innocent, and Sylvester the hungry everyman. And audiences identified with both. It is the dual purposes of these two characters that gets the audience to sympathize with them. It becomes almost impossible not to relate to one or the other, because each has something of a built-in secondary appeal. If we identify with Tweety, it isn't because we too are small and weak; it's because we too are smart and clever. If we identify with Sylvester, it isn't because we too are big, sloppy bullies; rather, it's because we too are hungry. Since each character is endowed with catchall traits, there isn't a viewer alive who can't relate to one or the other. And as trite as it sounds, there really is a little Tweety or Sylvester in each of us.

*Opposite: So close and yet so far: "Puddy Tats can't fly." **Above left:** Sylvester and Tweety in a rare friendly pose from "The Last Hungry Cat" (1961). **Above top and bottom:** Sylvester is on the cutting edge in both "Tree Cornered Tweety" (1956) and "Tweet, Tweet, Tweety" and gets bopped in "I Taw a Putty Tat" (1948).*

2
B.C.C.*
*(Before Cat and Canary)

Opposite: Tweety and Sylvester's often-repeated chase scenes were perfected by Mack Sennet's Keystone Kops. Charlie Chaplin's use of strong personality to create comedy exerted a powerful influence on the early animators.

The advent of sound in the movie business in the late 1920s signaled the end of the slapstick comedy tradition, but the great comic stars of the teens and early 1920s, including Charlie Chaplin, Harry Langdon, "Fatty" Arbuckle, and the Keystone Cops, were not forgotten.

One need only take a quick look at the live-action antics of these silent-film legends—Harold Lloyd hanging from a clock in "Safety Last" (1923), Buster Keaton being chased by a legion of policeman in "Cops" (1922), Charlie Chaplin dining on his shoe in "The Gold Rush" (1925)—to see the powerful influence they had on the early animators. Chaplin's style—his use of strong personality to create comedy—was particularly influential.

At the time, however, animation was more of a novelty than a respected art form. Max Fleischer and Walt Disney tried to attract attention to their cartoon creations by combining live action and animation (Disney's "Alice in Cartoonland" series; Fleischer's "Ko-Ko the Clown" series). Paul Terry designed spoofs of the legendary "Aesop's Fables," and other studios brought to "life" popular newspaper comic strips (Mutt and Jeff, Krazy Kat, the Katzenjammer

Sylvester's perils are just as real, and as funny, as the great gags created during comedy's silent film era. An example: Sylvester's leap to safety in "Daffy Duck's Quackbusters" (1988; bridging footage linking the film to the short "Hyde and Go Tweet") and a comparable sequence in Harold Lloyd's Safety Last.

Preceding pages: Theater day at Warner Bros. Cartoons.

Kids). Animator Otto Messmer injected some of Chaplin's personality into his Felix the Cat, having previously studied the Little Tramp for a series of early 1916 Chaplin cartoons.

This all changed in 1928, when Walt Disney introduced the world to Mickey Mouse. "Talkies" brought forth a new era in motion-picture entertainment, and musical cartoons became some of the most popular items on the bill. In 1930, Disney's star animators, Hugh Harmon and Rudolph Ising, brought their talking cartoon character Bosko to the attention of producer Leon Schlesinger. He, in turn, sold Warner Bros. on a series of musical cartoons that would promote popular songs in the Warner Bros. library. The series was called Looney Tunes and became so popular that a second series of "Merrie Melodies" began in 1931. The rest, as they say, is history.

LOONEY TUNES and MERRIE MELODIES

To keep up with the other studios, Warner Bros. needed a "star" cartoon character. Disney had Mickey Mouse, Paramount had Betty Boop and Popeye, Universal had Oswald the Rabbit. Although Bosko's cartoons were funny, something was missing. In 1933, Harmon and Ising left Schlesinger and took Bosko with them. Schlesinger quickly had his staff come up with a similar replacement: Buddy, a little song-and-dance man.

Something more was needed. In 1935, Schlesinger hired Fred "Tex" Avery (previously an animator at Walter Lantz) to head up a new unit of animators

Piggy (above) and Bosko (below) were the early stars of Looney Tunes and Merrie Melodies. **Right:** *Tex Avery shook up the status quo with cartoons like "Little Red Walking Hood" (1937) which featured this wacky wolf.*

HAM and EX

KITTY

OLIVER OWL

PORKY

BEANS

TOMMY TURTLE

Left: Model sheet of Warner's animated version of "Our Gang" introduced in Friz Freleng's "I Haven't Got a Hat" (1935). The following year, the boys from Termite Terrace (pictured above, left to right, Virgil Ross, Sid Sutherland, Tex Avery, Chuck Jones, and Bob Clampett) made a star out of Porky Pig. *Below:* Leon Schlesinger inserted his own picture in publicity art.

made up of younger, more radical artists (including Chuck Jones and Bob Clampett) who wanted to break the routine of musical shorts by making funnier, more adult cartoons. It is important to remember that animated cartoons made before 1958 were not aimed at children, but were intended for the entire moviegoing audience, adults included.

Avery's new unit took up residence in an old bungalow, separate from the rest of Schlesinger's animators. The bungalow-studio was dubbed "Termite Terrace" for the little chewing sounds coming from within the walls.

Life in the Termite Terrace was unlike that in any studio, in any field, anywhere. The animators of the Terrace adopted Avery's anything-for-a-laugh attitude as much in life as in their cartoons. As Bob Clampett told animation historian Mike Barrier, "Three-quarters of the fun at the cartoon studio wasn't on the screen." Caricatures of the boss and drawings of fellow animators in embarrassing situations were standard procedure among the artists. For a few years in the late 1930s, the staff created its own year-end gag reel featuring some of their wildest in-studio antics. One clip featured Avery, Jones, and Clampett dressing in drag to spoof the girls in the ink-and-paint department by sloshing paint onto the cels with huge paint brushes. Even Schlesinger's passion for the racetrack did not escape the camera's eye.

Termite Terrace soon produced Schlesinger's first true star, Porky Pig. Porky first appeared in Friz Freleng's 1935 Merrie Melody "I Haven't Got A Hat." Avery's team fashioned many cartoons around him over the years, including Frank Tashlin's "Porky's Romance" (1937), which introduced Porky's romantic interest, Petunia Pig. These cartoons also led to the introduction of another Merrie Melodies favorite, Daffy Duck, two years later.

HOW WARNER BROS. CARTOONS ARE ANIMATED

Making an animated film is a lot harder than many people think. The average seven minute Warner Bros. cartoon took between six and twelve months to produce, and required at least 5,000 separate drawings, the same number of cels, and about thirty finished background paintings.

The process begins when a storyman comes up with the general plot for a cartoon, and together with a sketch artist, proceeds to draw dozens of gags in little storyboard sketches. Next, the director reviews the storyboards, adds gags and takes out others. A final "jam session" is called with all storymen and directors and a script is finalized.

Then the voices are recorded and each word is handwritten onto "exposure sheets" to guide the animators on which frame of film will contain what dialogue. The director times the action frame by frame and assigns the scenes to his animators, after a layout artist has staged the action. Inkers place a cel over the finished pencil sketches and trace the characters with India ink. The inked cels are reversed and painters color them with opaque paints.

Meanwhile, the background artist, using the layout man's drawn models of the scenes, makes accurate paintings of each one. A stop-motion camera is used to shoot each cel in conjunction with the painted background. There are twenty-four frames of film shot for each second of screen time, between twelve and twenty-four animation drawings required for each second. The musical score is written to suit the mood of each part of the film; sound effects are added. All the elements are mixed in the final editing and the result is another hilarious Looney Tune or Merrie Melody.

Right: Animation drawing, background, and finished frame from "Birds of a Father," 1961. *Opposite:* Animation drawings and cels; thousands of these were made for each cartoon. *Bottom:* Sylvester in "Pappy's Puppy," 1955.

These photographs, taken in the 1950s, provide a step-by-step view of the creation of a cartoon in the Warner Bros. studio. *1.* Tedd Pierce, story man, prepares rough sketches for a storyboard. *2.* Warren Foster, also a story man, assembles his story sketches on a storyboard. *3.* Storyman Mike Maltese reviews a completed storyboard with director Chuck Jones. *4.* Maltese explains his story at a jam session, attended by directors, storymen, and animators, where gags are added, deleted, and refined. *5.* Director Friz Freleng and storyman Warren Foster review the story with animators before handing out the work to be animated. *6.* Mel Blanc (shown with director Robert McKimson) records the voices, following the finalized story. The animator is then guided by the dialogue for length and synchronization. *7.* Freleng, seated, plans the layout of the cartoon with his layout man, Hawley Pratt. *8.* Chuck Jones goes over backgrounds with background artist Phil DeGuard. *9.* Director Chuck Jones explains a point or two to animators Ken Harris and Ben Washam. *10.* Animator Ken Harris uses a mirror to create facial expression for Bugs Bunny. *11.* Twins Madilyn and Marilyn Wood, assistant animators, create the in-between animation-drawings. *12.* McKimson and his staff of animators study a pencil test on a Bugs Bunny scene. This test enables both directors and animators to spot any mistakes in timing, and make whatever corrections are necessary before the animation is prepared for final handling. *13.* McKimson and animator Rod Scribner run a piece of animation test film on a movieola machine. *14.* Before the animation is finally passed along for inking and painting, the animation is checked by checkers Paul Marron and Harry Love. *15.* After the animation is checked and okayed, the animation drawings (which are in

4

5

9

10

14

15

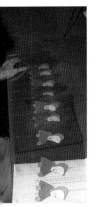

19

pencil and then marked for color) are sent to the Inking and Painting Department. *16.* Two inkers trace the pencil drawings with India ink onto sheets of celluloid. *17.* A painter now paints in the colors on the back of the cel; in this case, the cel is Sylvester. *18.* After the cels have been inked and painted, they are passed along for final checking to Esther Smith; here she is checking Granny cels. *19.* Cameraman Kenneth Moore shoots the cels against their proper background in continuity. There are usually twelve cels per second of cartoon time, and about thirty backgrounds for each cartoon. *20.* Carl Stalling, musical director, now writes the background music for the completed cartoon. *21.* After the cartoon has been photographed, the various scenes are put together in their continuity by film editor and sound effects man Treg Brown.

STRETCHING THE LIMITS

During the late 1930s the studio defined its style and came into its own. The humorously superior Warner Bros. cartoons began to surpass the at that time technically superior Disney cartoons in popularity. The films of Tex Avery, Bob Clampett, and other directors explored and expanded the limits of cartoon comedy. They broke the "fourth wall," talking back to the audience in films such as Avery's "Daffy Duck and Egghead" in which Eggy actually shoots a member of the audience. They began speeding up the timing of the animation and created such outrageously wacky characters as Daffy Duck and Bugs Bunny. Most notably, the studio established what was soon to become the sound of Warner Bros. cartoons: the music of Carl Stalling, and the voice of Mel Blanc.

All the experimentation of the 1930s, all the trial and error in creating this now-legendary studio, produced an experienced staff of laugh makers ready for the war-torn 1940s. In fact, the 1940s and 1950s were the golden age of Warner Bros. animation. The studio's unmatched creations were so consistently humorous that the appearance on the screen of the Warner Bros. shield became a sure sign to movie audiences that laughs were on the way.

During this period of superior production many of the now famous Warner Bros. characters came into being. Tweety and Sylvester had their debut, along with Yosemite Sam, Foghorn Leghorn, Pepe Le Pew, Speedy Gonzales, Hippety Hopper, Elmer Fudd, the Tazmanian Devil, the Road Runner, Wile E. Coyote, and many others.

Bugs Bunny was the most popular cartoon star of the 1940s. Joining him at Warner Bros. through the years were (opposite, clockwise): Elmer Fudd, Yosemite Sam, The Tasmanian Devil, Wile E. Coyote, Daffy Duck, Speedy Gonzales, Tweety, Sylvester, Sylvester, Jr., and Porky Pig. Center: Sylvester displays the motto of Warner Bros. cartoons in a scene from "Peck Up Your Troubles" (1945).

The unquestioned superstar of this madcap menagerie was Bugs Bunny. His anarchic spirit was the American spirit of the early 1940s. Some of the greatest cartoons of all time starred Bugs and have become classics—"What's Cookin' Doc?" (Clampett, 1944), in which Bugs disrupts the Academy Awards ceremony to campaign for an Oscar; "A Hare Grows in Brooklyn" (Freleng, 1947), which recounts Bugs' youth in Brooklyn; "Gorilla My Dreams" (McKimson, 1948), in which Bugs gets even with an ape who adopts him against his will; "Rabbit of Seville" (Jones, 1950), in which Elmer chases Bugs onto an opera stage.

Running a close second in popularity to the lovable wiseguy Bugs Bunny was the uncontrolled lunatic Daffy Duck. In "Daffy—The Commando" (Freleng, 1943), Daffy bops Hitler on the head with a mallet. In "The Great Piggy Bank Robbery" (Clampett, 1946), Daffy imagines himself as Duck Twacy, Detective. Some of his more creative roles included that of a "mustache maniac" graffiti artist in "Daffy Doodles" (McKimson, 1946), and a zany quiz-show host in "The Ducksters" (Jones, 1950).

But while Bugs and Daffy, were undeniably popular, it was Tweety and Sylvester who quietly stole the show in 1947 by winning Warner Bros. its first Academy Award.

3
THE EARLY BIRDS

clever, defenseless canary and a conniving, failure of a cat. Where did the idea for the cat vs. bird chase hatch? Like most of the characters in Warner Bros. cartoons, they were results of the studio's creative and collaborative set-up. At Warner Bros., the simple plot of a cat chasing a bird dates back to a 1935 cartoon called "Billboard Frolics" in which an alley cat pursues a little bird that has come to life from a billboard advertisement. But the real inspiration for the match-up came from 1941's "The Cagey Canary," co-directed by Tex Avery and Bob Clampett.

Written by Michael Maltese and dealing with a cat's attempts to a catch a clever canary without being heard by a "Granny" who is sleeping upstairs is the classic domestic "Tweety and Sylvester" plot in its earliest and simplest form. Avery and his unit began the film, and it was completed by Clampett when Avery left the studio.

Frank Tashlin then picked up on this domestic cat vs. bird situation for his 1943 film "Puss n' Booty," in which Rudolph the house cat meets his match in the cage-bound Petey bird. (This basic story was remade by Friz Freleng as the 1948 Tweety and Sylvester cartoon "I Taw a Putty Tat.")

Bob Clampett went in another direction with the innocent bird scenario when he and his team began developing a funny little bird in 1942. Intended as a supporting player, "Orson," as he was called on the studio model sheets,

Preceding pages, above and below: Animation art and background from Avery and Clampett's "The Cagey Canary" (1941), the cartoon that established the classic Tweety/Sylvester chase situation.

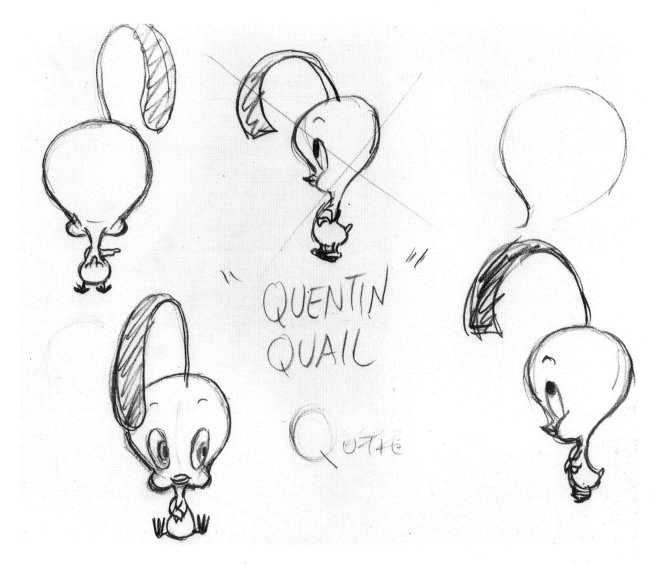

first appeared in the black-and-white Looney Tune "Wacky Blackout" in a bit part as a sickly little baby bird who surprises his mom with his desire to become a "dive bomber" to help the war effort.

A BIRD IS HATCHED

Later that year, Clampett decided to spoof Abbott and Costello, America's most popular comedy team, in a cartoon film. "A Tale of Two Kitties" featured the pair as a couple of bird-hungry cats. Along with the amusing caricatures of Bud and Lou as "Babbit" and "Catstello," the film also pokes fun at such World War II homefront activities as air raids, blackouts, and victory gardens. But it was the appearance of the little bird who says, "I tawt I taw a puddy tat!" that really stole the show. Clampett originated that signature line himself, after a doodle he made up in the mid-1930s. Clampett had written a letter on MGM stationery to a musician friend, and next to the picture of the MGM lion he had scribbled a little bird saying in a word balloon, "I tink I taw a titty-tat." The line became a running gag between the two friends, and when Bob had the opportunity to use it (albeit slightly altered) in Tweety's first cartoon, he did. That line, along with Tweety's antics in the first cartoon, created an overnight sensation. "I saw one of your cartoons downtown with *Casablanca*. It was the

Above: These Clampett designs for Quentin Quail were never used.
Below: In-between drawing from Tweety's first scene in "A Tale of Two Kitties" (1942).

*"A Tale of Two Kitties" was a takeoff on America's most popular comedy stars, Abbot and Costello. Tweety stole the show. **Below:** Pencil sketch of publicity art. **Opposite:** Frames.*

one about two pussy cats. I thought it was very clever. I particularly liked the little bird." This quote from a letter by Margaret Maas is typical of the incredible response that met this first Tweety cartoon.

In "A Tale of Two Kitties," Tweety's personality is somewhat extreme and aggressive. The character is deceptively innocent when first reacting to the putty tats ("Poor puddytat, he cwushed his wittle head!"), but later he plays "This Little Piggy" while removing Catstello's claws from a clothesline ten stories up. Most of the humor comes from the little bird's violent come-backs to the cats' attacks. Tweety uses bats, slingshots, anvils, and dynamite to protect his nest during the course of the cartoon, finally calling up the "4th Interceptor Command" to shoot down the slingshot-propelled putty tat as enemy aircraft.

"Sometimes a character comes to you in one night," Clampett said, "and other times it comes in tiny individual pieces like a jigsaw puzzle that finally comes together in one magical moment. In school I remember seeing nature films which showed newborn birds in a nest. They always looked funny to me. This stuck in my mind: the helpless bird in a nest. One time I kicked around the idea of a twin pair of baby birds called "Twick 'n' Tweet" who were precursors of Tweety."

My "FIRST" "Tweety" CARTOON —

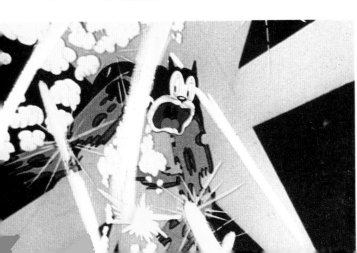

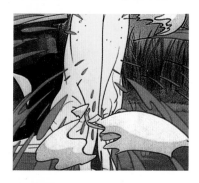

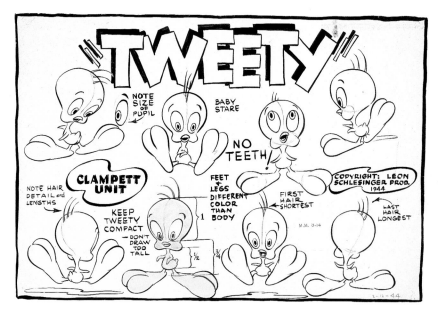

Examples of Clampett's aggressive Tweety in "Birdy and the Beast. **Above and right:** *Frames.* **Opposite:** *Storyboard sketches by Rod Scribner.* **Above right:** *Model sheet by Tom McKimson, who later created the first sketch of Tweety and Sylvester as a pair, showing their relative sizes.*

Tweety's next appearance not only offered him star billing but gave him his name. Clampett's "Birdy and the Beast" (1944) pits the little bird against a potbellied cat looking for dinner. The bird's personality is toned down a bit and is somewhat more innocent than in the previous film. Tweety uses the cat's tongue as a blanket. Then, when it suddenly gets dark, he lights a match to see where he is—a match that in turn starts a blaze inside the poor cat's mouth. The bird causes more than his share of intentional trouble in this film: leading the cat to disturb a mean bulldog, smashing a face full of chicken eggs in his mouth, and finally handing the cat a live hand grenade.

It became obvious that the key to the humor and charm of Tweety was in making him sweeter. The set-up for the gags was his innocence, the pay-off his aggression. Clampett has a wonderful moment in the film when Tweety whistles and dances to a theme-song melody, a moment that serves no other purpose than to show off the character's innocence and purity.

In "A Gruesome Twosome," the previously pink Tweety became a yellow feathered canary. Bob Clampett recalled that movie censors objected to Tweety because he looked naked. Rather than take the suggestion of giving his character a pair of short pants, Clampett gave Tweety yellow feathers.

The gruesome twosome themselves are two alley cats (one a caricature of comedian Jimmy Durante, the other a dim-witted goof), both rivals for the attention of a female feline. The first cat to bring her a little bird will win her hand, so a competition ensues. Unfortunately for our catty friends, the bird

TWEETY TAKES PIN OUT OF GRENADE

TWEETY PUSHES GRENADE UNDER CAT'S HAND—

HELP- OUCH! UNHAND ME—! YOU BRUTE!

CAT TAKES GRENADE

OH BOY! OH BOY! OH BOY!

OUT OF TREE

I GOT IT- I GOT IT! I GOT IT

HE DOT IT—AN' HE TAN' HAVE IT!

TWEETY VERY NONCHALANT —

BOB CLAMPETT

Bob Clampett (1913-1984) was one of the pioneers of American animation. While still in his teens, he designed the first Mickey Mouse doll; shortly thereafter he joined the Harman-Ising studios and animated scenes for the first Merrie Melodie ever made, "Lady Play Your Mandolin." In 1935, Clampett was assigned as animator and key gagman to director Tex Avery and his team at "Termite Terrace." Avery and Clampett forged a new direction in cartoons by displaying a wild, irreverent sense of humor that later became known as the Warner style. In 1937, Clampett was promoted to Director and during the next nine years he directed some of the funniest, wildest, and most memorable cartoons in animation history—among them "Porky in Wackyland" (1938); "Corny Concerto" "Coal Black and de Sebben Dwarfs" (1943); and "The Great Piggy Bank Robbery" (1946). Clampett was also instrumental in the creation and development of Porky Pig, Daffy Duck, and Bugs Bunny. He introduced Tweety Bird, patterned on his own nude baby picture, in "A Tale of Two Kitties."

Below: Bob Clampett detested this nude baby picture all through his childhood; it later became the model for Tweety."

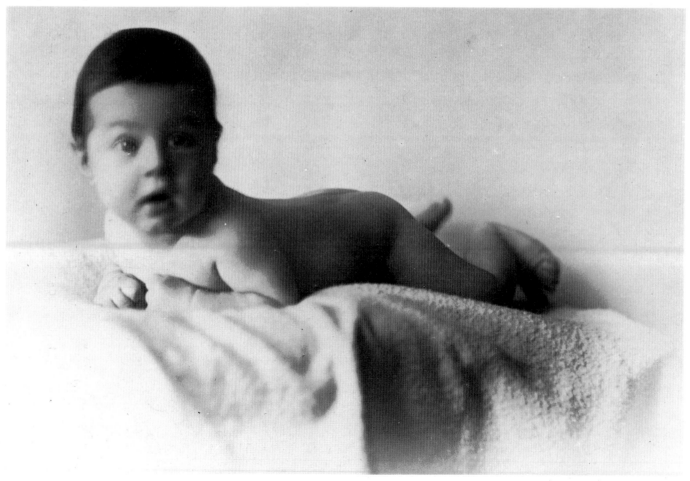

40

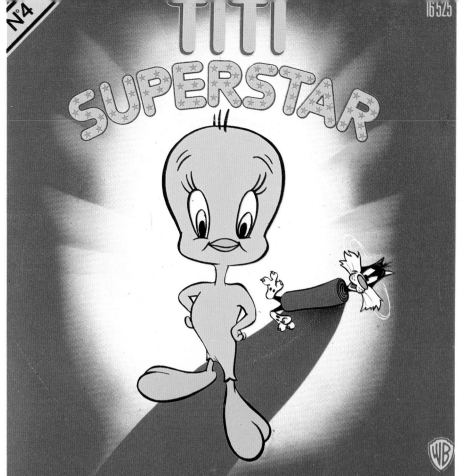

*Above: When Clampett left the Warner Studio in 1946, he opened his studio and created the popular Beany and Cecil. **Right:** Tweety became a superstar in France in the 1970s. **Below:** Limited edition artwork from "Porky in Wacky-land," a Clampett classic.*

*Below: Frames from "A Gruesome Twosome." **Opposite:** Model sheet by Tom McKimson shows original design of "Durante" cat and other supporting players.*

they go after is Tweety. Tweety counterattacks throughout the film, abusing not only the poor puddy tats, but smacking a bulldog around with a bone and slapping an angry bumblebee silly.

A CAT IS LET OUT OF THE BAG

"Sufferin' succotash!" were the first words uttered by the hungry alley cat introduced in Friz Freleng's "Life with Feathers" (1945). Unlike most cartoon stars of the golden age, Sylvester the cat arrived on the screen a completed character, behaving almost exactly the way he did in his first appearance as he would for the next twenty years of short subjects.

Since they were hoping to hit upon the right ingredients for stardom, it usually took time for the Warner animators to fine-tune the on-screen personalities of their characters. Although Sylvester was tweaked a bit in his subsequent films (his white fur is gray in Freleng's 1945 "Peck Up Your Troubles,"

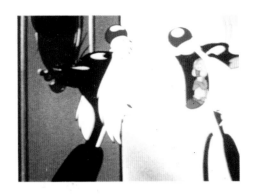

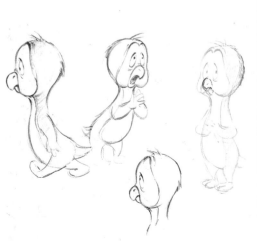

Sylvester's first two appearances in 1945: "Life with Feathers" (above and below) and "Peck Up Your Troubles" (right).

and in the two 1948 Arthur Davis cartoons "Doggone Cats" and "Catch as Cats Can" Sylvester looks the same but has a completely different character), the animators eventually came back around to their original thinking. The finishing touch for Sylvester was just that—the name Sylvester. This name was first used in Chuck Jones's 1948 cartoon "Scaredy Cat" (he was unnamed in all previous cartoons except "Tweetie Pie," in which he was called "Thomas").

Friz Freleng says that while he was working with layout artist Hawley Pratt, "I designed Sylvester to look subtly like a clown. I gave him a big red nose and a very low crotch, which was supposed to look like he was wearing baggy pants. But gradually he was changed, because the construction restricted his animation." Sylvester's voice came from "the sound of Warner Bros.," Mel Blanc, and the voice Blanc used for the "big sloppy cat" was actually the same one he used for Daffy Duck's earlier voice, only it wasn't speeded, as Daffy's was. As Robert McKimson says of Sylvester, "He had a juicy voice, you know. He's the closest, I would say, that Mel would come to have an original voice and then

fitting the character to it. Of course, Daffy Duck's voice is the same as Sylvester's, only sped. So I guess when Mel recorded Daffy, it sounded like Sylvester."

In his Academy-Award-nominated debut film, "Life with Feathers," Sylvester is a starving pussycat who is suspicious of a parakeet that wants to be eaten, and he goes to great lengths to keep the bird out of his mouth.

Sylvester's troubles are more typical in his next film, Friz Freleng's "Peck Up Your Troubles," in which he chases a woodpecker. It is apparent from even his earliest cartoons that Sylvester's destiny was the pursuit of birds, and one particular bird was soon to make Sylvester a household word.

Bob Clampett used Sylvester as the leader of a group of housecats determined not to be left out on a cold winter night in "Kitty Kornered" (1946). "It's uncatstitutional!" spits Sylvester in a speech rather emotional for a cat. This hilarious battle of wits with homeowner Porky Pig reaches its high point when the cats disguise themselves as men from Mars to scare Porky into running from his home.

Friz Freleng's cartoons are different in style from those of Bob Clampett. Clampett pushed cartooning to the edge, made extensive use of topical humor, and did just about anything for a laugh. The more conservative Freleng generally used the more controlled structure of traditional comedy filmmaking. When Clampett left Warner Bros. in 1946, he was working on Tweety's next cartoon, pairing him with the cat (later named Sylvester by storyman Tedd Pierce who thought that a lisping character needed a sibilant name).

"When I saw Clampett's Tweety pictures, I saw something in them I would like to do," recalls Friz Freleng. "There were things about Bob Clampett that I admired. He was innovative and he dared . . . He dared a lot."

Above and above Left: Freleng came up with a woodpecker to heckle in "Peck Up Your Troubles" before Tweety replaced him for good in "Tweetie Pie." Meanwhile, Clampett teamed Porky and Sylvester for the first time in the hilarious "Kitty Kornered" (below).

FRIZ FRELENG

Chuck Jones has written: "No student of animation can safely ignore the wizardry of Freleng's cartoons—if he can stop laughing long enough to seriously study their beauty." The hot-tempered Yosemite Sam, the innocent canary bird Tweety, and the conniving alley cat Sylvester all owe their hilarious careers to the talents of Isadore "Friz" Freleng. Friz began animating for Walt Disney in the 1920s and joined Warner Bros. in 1930, receiving screen credit on their very first cartoon, "Sinkin' in the Bathtub." Though he specialized in musical cartoons like "The Three Little Bops," "Rhapsody in Rivets," and "Rhapsody Rabbit," Friz was also instrumental in developing the personalities of Daffy Duck, Speedy Gonzales, Tweety, and Sylvester. Freleng directed the first cartoon featuring Porky Pig in 1935, and has directed a record 62 Bugs Bunny shorts. In 1963, Friz teamed with producer David DePatie to form DePatie-Freleng Enterprises, which created the Pink Panther. Freleng's cartoons have won a total of four Academy Awards, including those won for "Tweetie Pie" and "Speedy Gonzales."

Below: Limited edition artwork.
Opposite: Animation drawing from "Rhapsody Rabbit," 1946, a Freleng masterpiece.

BIRD MEETS CAT

Freleng's own version of Tweety came in "Tweetie Pie." "I made him look more like a charming baby, with a bigger head and big blue eyes," said Freleng. "He's a canary because we say he's a canary. . . . He doesn't look like a canary. We didn't have time to develop characters. When you see Yosemite Sam, you know he's a villain, when you see Tweety the audience is sympathetic." Aware that Tweety needed adversaries, Clampett provided him with strong characters

*Opposite: Gags from "Tweetie Pie": Tweety is taken in from the cold and meets Sylvester for the first time; Sylvester ties an electric fan to his body, which, in perfect cartoon logic, enables him to fly (until Tweety pulls the plug on him); Sylvester climbs on metal chairs to reach the birdcage while Tweety finds a handy blowtorch to pull him down. **Right:** Cel from "Tweetie Pie."*

to play against. In "Tweetie Pie," Tweety is matched with "Thomas" (Sylvester), a housecat with culinary plans for the new pet bird. With both of the character's personalities now honed to perfection, and with a great collection of chase gags masterfully executed, "Tweetie Pie" won raves from moviegoing audiences and from the motion picture industry as well. The film won the Academy Award for best animated short subject in 1947—the first Oscar for the Warner Bros. cartoon studio.

Oddly, Sylvester was never meant to be permanently matched with Tweety. His character was much too versatile for that. But after the success of "Tweetie Pie," Freleng was convinced that Tweety couldn't work without Sylvester. To Freleng and the rest of the world, the two were a match made in cartoon heaven.

4
WONDER YEARS

The enormous success of the first teaming of Tweety and Sylvester is attested to by the fact that even today people often refer to Tweety as "Tweety Pie," which was the title of their first cartoon and was nothing more than a pun on the loving expression "sweetie pie."

The film "Tweetie Pie" solidified the personalities of both characters, at least as far as the Freleng unit was concerned. The two characters were never directed by any of the other units as a pair, although Sylvester was used by other directors. The year 1948 saw the release of Chuck Jones's version of Sylvester in "Scaredy Cat," and the cat had his first encounter with a "giant mouse" named Hippety Hopper in Robert McKimson's "Hop, Look and Listen." Jones created a unique personality for Sylvester in "Scaredy Cat," completely different and totally hilarious. Sylvester is a silent, timid, and scared pussycat companion to Porky Pig as they spend their first night in their new home—a gothic mansion haunted by dozens of killer mice. All sorts of nightmarish things begin happening around the duo—Porky's bed is rolled out the window, and knives, anvils, arrows, and bowling balls are dropped or thrown at the unknowing pig. Unfortunately for Sylvester, he is the only one of the pair that is aware of the reality of the situation. The cat saves his master at every turn, but Porky inevitably wakes up just in time to see Sylvester alone with the weapons, seemingly the source of the trouble. Jones thus added his own brand of intellectual humor.

Sylvester meets more confusion in McKimson's "Hop, Look and Listen," which introduced Hippety Hopper, a boxing kangaroo who escapes from the zoo. Sylvester believes he's got a giant mouse in the house. This scenario became

Above: An early animation drawing of Sylvester. *Below: Two model sheets of Tweety from 1947: from "Tweetie Pie," (left) and a revised version from "Bad Ol' Putty Tat."*

STORYMEN

The storyman's job was to come up with the plots and gags for the cartoons, and to draw the storyboards themselves or with a story sketch artists. The storyboard consists of many small drawings pinned to a corkboard which give the directors and animators an overview of the film at a glance. The chief storymen at Warner Bros. during the golden age were Michael Maltese, Tedd Pierce, and Warren Foster.

Below: Storyboard sketches by Rod Scribner from Bob Clampett's "Birdy and the Beast," 1944.
Bottom: Tedd Pierce points out gags in the storyboard for a Bugs Bunny cartoon while Michael Maltese acts it out. In the audience: Bob Clampett, Warren Foster, Friz Freleng, and Robert McKimson.

WHISTLES

BRRRR
TWEETY SHIVERS

TWEETY PULLS CAT'S TONGUE OVER HIM LIKE A BLANKET—

"SYLVESTER"

© WARNER BROS.
CARTOONS INC.
47

Sylvester in the 1940s: **top :** *A model sheet based on animation from "Tweetie Pie."* **Above:** *Animation art from "Pop 'Im Pop!"*

popular with McKimson, and he repeated it with minor variations throughout his career.

Meanwhile, Friz Freleng kept Sylvester busy chasing Tweety into a variety of funny situations. In "Bad Ol' Putty Tat" (1949) Tweety lives atop a birdhouse perched on a twenty-five-foot-high pole covered in barbed wire. Sylvester's efforts to snatch the bird using a girdle as a trampoline prove useless in the face of Tweety's own use of dynamite. In "Home Tweet Home" (1950)Tweety outsmarts Sylvester by hiding on top of the cat's head! ("He'll never find me here!"); "All A-Bir-r-r-d" (1950) puts the chase aboard a locomotive, with Sylvester trying to catch Tweety in the baggage car but getting pummeled in the caboose by another traveler—a bulldog; and in "Canary Row" (1950) Sylvester disguises himself as an organ-grinder monkey, bellboy, and tightrope walker in efforts to gain access to Tweety in the Broken Arms Hotel where there are "no cats allowed."

NEW FACES, NEW PLACES

The basic structure of the Tweety and Sylvester cartoons remained the same throughout the 1950s. Only the locales of the chase changed. The essential tale has the hungry Sylvester spotting Tweety and then making clever attempts to

LAYOUTS AND BACKGROUNDS

Layout artists are the cartoon directors' "right hand men." They design the overall look of a particular cartoon, and plan how each scene is to appear and be animated. After the storyboards are completed, the layout artist, working with the director, will design the backgrounds for each shot, determine how and where characters will enter and move through the scene, and plan camera moves.

Hawley Pratt was Friz Freleng's layout man from "Tweetie Pie" through the close of the studio. Robert McKimson used many layout artists, including Robert Givens, Cornett Wood, and Robert Gribbroek.

Background painters are true unsung heroes in animation. They are fine artists who must work fast to create full painted backgrounds which convey the proper settings and mood for every scene in the film—and in a zany Warner Bros. cartoon, that can mean thirty to fifty paintings for each cartoon. Often these backgrounds contained well-turned gags.

Warner Bros. utilized the talents of Richard H. Thomas, Paul Julian, Peter Alvarado, Philip DeGuard, Irv Wyner, Boris Gorelick, Bill Butler, and Tom O'Loughlin for their backgrounds.

A7 PUDC⊻ 7AT ⊂HⅭⅢℇ KNℇⅢⅢ
1E 7ANT FWⅢ !

Above: Storyboard sketches from
Chuck Jones' *Satan's Waitin'.*

THE OTHER SIDE OF THE TRACKS

The soundtrack of an animated cartoon is just as important to the film as the artwork. The two people most responsible for the unique sound of Warner Bros. cartoons are voice actor Mel Blanc and musician Carl Stalling. Both were an integral part of the Looney Tunes factory, inspiring their colleagues and influencing their success.

Mel Blanc, the voice of Sylvester and Tweety, was born May 30, 1908 in San Francisco. Establishing a career in radio in Los Angeles during the 1930s, Mel soon branched into voice-over work in the movies, most notably in animated cartoons. Mel did voices for every animation studio in the late thirties, but got his best parts at Warner Bros. Starting at Termite Terrace in 1936, Mel quickly refashioned Porky Pig's annoying stutter into a humorous vocalization. After making distinctive contributions to Daffy Duck and Bugs Bunny, Mel was awarded an exclusive contract, and screen credit, for his voice characterizations.

In his autobiography, Mel Blanc recounted his work with Sylvester: "Sylvester has always been a favorite of mine. He's always been the easiest character for me to play. When I was first shown the model sheet of Sylvester, with his floppy jowls and generally disheveled appearance, I said to Friz Freleng, 'A big sloppy cat should have a big *shthloppy* voice. He should spray even more than Daffy.' While recording Sylvester cartoons, my scripts would get so covered with saliva I'd repeatedly have to wipe them clean. I used to suggest to actress June Foray, who played Tweety's vigilant owner Granny, that she wear a raincoat to the sessions."

Blanc borrowed a line from one of his other vocal creations, traveling salesman Roscoe E. Wortle from radio's "The Judy Canova Show," for use with Sylvester: "Thufferin' thuccatash!"

Carl Stalling came into the cartoon world through his association with Walt Disney. Stalling, who had been a theater organist in Disney's hometown of Kansas City, was brought to Hollywood to become Disney's first musical director in 1928. Stalling soon joined Ub Iwerks ("Flip the Frog") studio in the 1930s and made his way to Warner Bros. the same time as Mel Blanc, 1936.

Stalling had a genius for mixing popular songs, classical themes, and original music together to create a soundtrack as funny as the films themselves. Stalling told Mike Barrier in a 1969 interview: "The musicians said they enjoyed the cartoons more than anything else. They looked forward to coming down to record the cartoons. It was screwy stuff, you know."

Stalling retired in 1957 after having scored over 600 Warner Bros. cartoons.

Opposite: Sylvester and Tweety
were the inspiration for a platinum
record, sung by Mel Blanc, in 1950.

catch the bird that end in disaster and provide the laughs. Still, Freleng was able to make each cartoon unique, creating film after hilarious film. As Bob Baker wrote in "Film Dope" in 1982, "The Sylvester and Tweety confrontations provide the richest seam in Freleng's golden age. Within a rigorously restricted format, Freleng engineered the most delicate series of elaborations and variations, finally turning Sylvester into the patron saint of obsessives and masochists. These films contributed a great deal to the history of hilarity; there was never anything quite like them at the time (even within the Warner setup) and there has never been anything quite like them since."

As the series progressed in the 1950s, Tweety fell into the role of spectator. According to Friz Freleng, "They became Sylvester pictures, rather than Tweety pictures." Freleng elaborated in a 1982 interview with Lewis Archi-

Tweety and Sylvester in their prime. **Opposite:** *Granny thwarts Sylvester's latest scheme in "Gift Wrapped" (1952). Her punchline: "Ya didn't count on Pocahontas, did ya, Geronimo?"* **Above:** *Animation drawing from "All Abird-r-r-d" (1950).* **Above right:** *Storyboard sketches from "Tweety's Circus," (1955)* **Below right:** *Storyboard sketches from "Satan's Waitin'" (1955).*

bald in *The Aquarian*: "Tweety doesn't do anything. He can't even put a hat on because his arms are too short. And he's got such a big head. The comedy comes out of Sylvester and his determination, his stubbornness to get this bird no matter what happens to him. Still, everybody says, 'Oh, I love that Tweety.'' Audiences are funny. They never love the characters that really get the laughs.'"

Sylvester's determination is seen in another character who was developed by Chuck Jones—Wile E. Coyote, whose prey was the ever-elusive Road Runner. Freleng has acknowledged that Sylvester was his own coyote.

But unlike the Road Runner series, which was more or less restricted to the desert, Tweety and Sylvester weren't bound to Granny's house. The locales of the cartoons were varied and provided new opportunities for gags. The Tweety and Sylvester chases spanned the globe, everywhere from the backyard to the Old West, from the circus to the zoo. In "Tweety's S.O.S" (1951) they chase around an ocean liner. On board, Tweety's attempt to cure Sylvester's sudden sea sickness with "a nice, juicy piece of salt pork" sends the pussycat running to the infirmary. Early in "Greedy for Tweety" (1957) Sylvester, Tweety, and

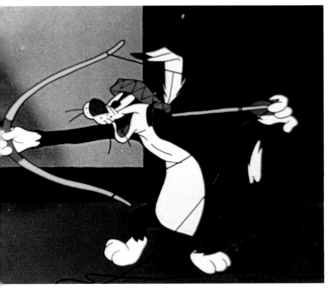

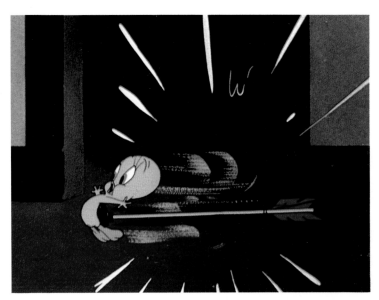

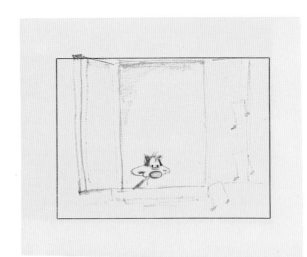

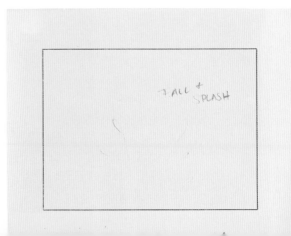

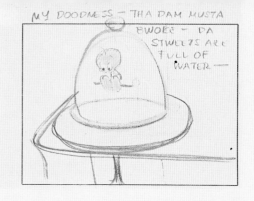

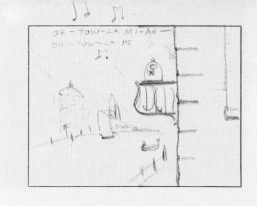

a bulldog have broken legs in casts at the local hospital (cared for by nurse Granny). Their plight doesn't stop the trio from trying to kill one another. When Granny finds Tweety missing and Sylvester burping yellow feathers, she performs an operation that gets Tweety back to his cage and leaves Sylvester with a patch on his stomach.

At the beach in "Sandy Claws" (1955), Sylvester plays lifeguard as he tries to rescue Tweety when the little bird gets stranded on an off-shore rock. Instead of being pummeled by the bulldog, the cat, at every attempt at the canary, gets his knocks from a hungry shark. And it's Italy in "A Pizza Tweety Pie" (1958), which features a Neapolitan Sylvester ("Sooferin' a soocatasha!") chasing tourist Tweety through the canals of Venice.

During the 1950s, poor Sylvester had new problems to contend with in addition to his usual frustrations from his feathered friend. Hippety Hopper made matters worse for Sylvester, embarrassing the poppa pussycat in front of his very own son, Junior. Introduced in 1950's "Pop 'Im Pop," Sylvester Junior was quite often responsible for sending his dad into some of his most painful situations, pitting him against the kangaroo mistaken for a giant mouse ("C'mon, Pop! Go get the mouse like you said you could, unless you want to destroy a child's faith in his father!").

In the Academy Award-winning cartoon "Speedy Gonzales" (1955), Sylvester meets the fastest mouse in all Mexico, "a friend of everyone's sister," who subjects the cat to such indignities as causing him to fall into a dozen carefully placed mouse traps. Speedy runs full speed into Sylvester's mouth only to race through the cat and pop out his tail!

*The many colors of Sylvester. **Left, top to bottom:** "Ain't She Tweet" (1952); "Tweet and Lovely" (1959); "Scaredy Cat" (1948); "Gonzales Tamales" (1957). **Above:** "Mouse and Garden" (1963). **Preceding pages:** Storyboard sketches from "A Pizza Tweety Pie."*

ANIMATORS

It's the animator's job to make the characters live and breathe, to give them personality through movement and to draw the main poses which will put across the gags outlined on the storyboards.

The main animators in Friz Freleng's unit during the Tweety years included Gerry Chiniquy, a personality animator who was best at drawing cantankerous characters like Granny and Yosemite Sam; Ken Champin, one of the best animators at putting gags across; Virgil Ross, who specialized in action scenes, Manuel Perez, and Art Davis, known, along with Rod Scribner, for his wild takes and cartoony animation style. The main animators in McKimson's unit during his early Hippety Hopper days include Charles McKimson, Phil DeLara, and Rod Scribner; later animators included Keith Darling, Ted Bonnicksen, George Grandpre, Russ Dyson, and Warren Batchelder.

Below: Animators' worksheet from Clampett's "A Gruesome Twosome," 1945.

Right: Animation drawings by Virgil Ross from "Little Red Rodent Hood," 1952.

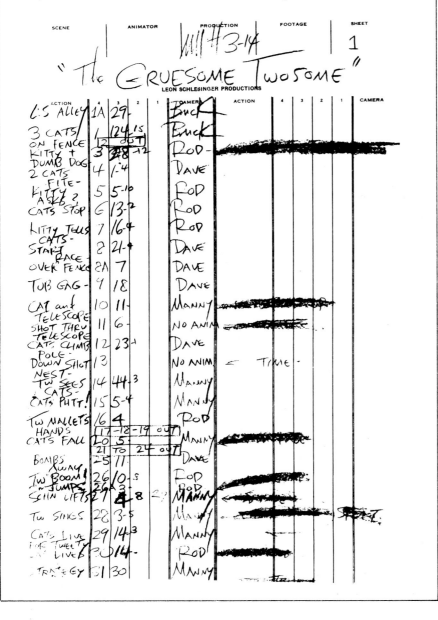

63

ROBERT McKIMSON

As the creator of the Tasmanian Devil, Foghorn Leghorn, and Hippety Hopper, Robert McKimson was one of the chief wizards behind the classic Warner Bros. cartoons. McKimson began his career in 1928 at Walt Disney's Oswald Rabbit studio. When Disney left to produce Mickey Mouse, McKimson joined fellow Oswald animators Hugh Harmon and Rudolf Ising, teaming with producer Leon Schlesinger, to make Looney Tunes and Merrie Melodies for Warner Bros. He remained at Warner Bros. for the next 32 years. During his career at Warner's, McKimson earned praise as the studio's best animator and character designer, and rose from the ranks to join Chuck Jones and Friz Freleng in the triumvirate of senior directors at the studio from 1946 onward. In addition to the characters named above, McKimson also made many of the best cartoons starring Bugs Bunny, Daffy Duck, Porky Pig, Speedy Gonzales, and Sylvester.

Below: Publicity drawing by
Robert McKimson.

STARDOM AND RERUNS

Tweety and Sylvester acted in an important series of cartoons for Warner Bros. into the early 1960s. "Birds Anonymous" (1957) became the series' second Oscar-winning cartoon. A parody of Alcoholics Anonymous, this film finds Sylvester joining "B.A." to kick the bird habit—but doing so makes him a nervous wreck. After all, as Tweety notes, "Once a bad 'ol putty tat, always a bad 'ol putty tat!" Freleng tried some twists in the series, for example putting the characters in such fairy tales as "Red Riding Hoodwinked" (1955) and "Tweety and the Beanstalk" (1957). In the latter, Sylvester climbs the beanstalk only to find a giant canary ("Acres and acres of Tweety bird, and it's mine! All mine!"). He winds up in giant trouble. Another twist entailed fashioning some films after popular television series. In "Tree Cornered Tweety" (1956) Tweety narrates the cartoon a la monotoned Jack Webb in "Dragnet" ("This

Tweety and Sylvester in the 1960s.
Above: *A ridiculous team-up of Sylvester and Wile E. Coyote in "The Wild Chase" (1965).*
Below: *Model sheets from 1960s cartoons.*

Right: Tweety's popularity in France (where he was called "Titi") is evidenced by this collection of memorabilia.

Tweety and Sylvester on television. **Right:** *Co-starring with Bugs Bunny and his ABC network prime time series.* **Below:** *Later, co-starring on Saturday morning.*

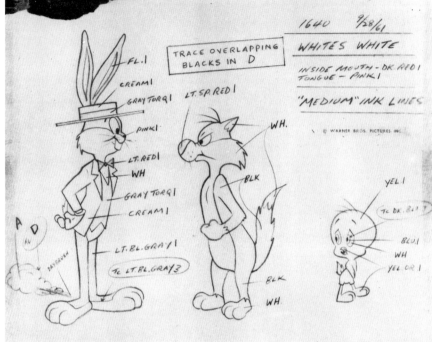

is the city. Three million people. Three hundred thousand putty tats. That's where I come in. I'm a little bird. I live in a cage. My name is Tweety."). "The Last Hungry Cat" (1961) parodies "Alfred Hitchcock Presents" as it focuses on Sylvester as he slowly goes mad over the possibility of finally eating Tweety.

Before the Warner cartoon studio was completely phased out in the 1960s, Tweety and Sylvester made frequent appearances on "The Bugs Bunny Show" (1960-62, ABC). The older films began replaying on television during this decade and created a new wave of interest in the Warner Bros. cartoons around the world.

Tweety became a national fad in France in 1975. Called "Titi" in French, two compilations of old Tweety shorts grossed over $1 million in that country. Back in the United States, Tweety and Sylvester gained a network Saturday morning show of their own on CBS in 1976. Sylvester became the spokesperson for 9-Lives cat foods in 1980. The characters have been featured in numerous Warner Bros. cartoon television specials and Bugs Bunny feature-length compilation films. "The Bugs Bunny & Tweety Show" began on ABC in 1986 and continues to this day.

CHUCK JONES

Known as the "intellectual" of the Warner Bros. directors, Chuck Jones began his career in the early 1930s as a cel washer at Ub Iwerks studio. He advanced to animator at Warner Bros., and joined the Termite Terrace crew. Promoted to director in 1938, Jones was instrumental in developing Bugs Bunny, Elmer Fudd, and Daffy Duck, as well as in setting the fast-paced tone of Warner Bros. cartoons in general. He also created Henery Hawk, Pepe Le Pew, Marvin Martian, Wile E. Coyote, and the Roadrunner. He directed four Sylvester cartoons; they are among the funniest in the series. Steven Spielberg has called Jones, "a comic genius up there with Keaton and Chaplin."

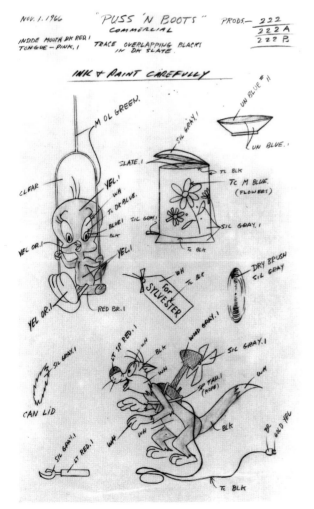

© Warner Bros. Inc. 1979

9-Lives
Dry Cat Food®

Tweety and Sylvester continued to entertain while endorsing Puss 'N' Boots and 9-Lives cat foods.

Right: Merchandise based on Tweety and Sylvester are highly-valued collectibles, including drinking glasses, dolls, and statue by Mark Wallace. *Below:* Tweety Halloween costume, circa 1965. *Right:* Comic books produced from 1975 on.

LIMITED EDITION CELS

Limited editions cels (such as the ones at right by Friz Freleng and the one below by Bob Clampett Productions) have become enormously popular and increasingly valuable; Chuck Jones and the heirs of Robert McKimson create them as well as Freleng and the Clampett heirs. Often based on original animation art or scenes, they are available in fine art and animation galleries. For more information about acquiring them:

Animation Plus! Gallery, 8610 West Third Street, Los Angeles, CA 90048, 213-275-5513, 790 North Milwaukee Avenue, River West, Chicago, IL 60622, 312-243-8666

Circle Galleries, 303 W. Wacker Street, Suite 830, Chicago, IL 60601 (800-PLAN-ART)

Bob Clampett Productions, 729 Seward Street, Los Angeles, CA 90038

Gallery Lainzberg, 200 Guaranty Building, Cedar Rapids, Iowa 52401, 800-553-9995

Howard Lowery Gallery, 3818 West Magnolia Boulevard, Burbank, CA 91505

Toon Art Galleries, 1133 North Dearborn, Suite 1609, Chicago, IL 60610

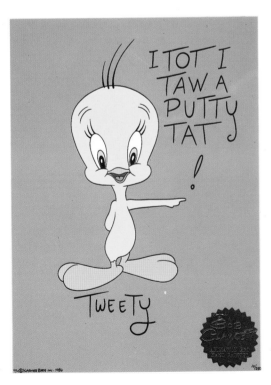

Warner Bros. keeps Tweety and Sylvester alive with video cassette releases, continuing appearances on TV specials and feature films. **Bottom right:** *Sylvester in "Bugs Bunny's Overtures to Disaster," (1991).* **Opposite:** *"Bugs Bunny's Christmas Carol" (top, 1980) and Friz Freleng's Looney, Looney, Looney Bugs Bunny Movie (bottom, 1981).* **Below:** *Segment from the Bugs Bunny comic strip written by Brett Koth, drawn by Shawn Keller.*

Chuck Jones, Friz Freleng, and the heirs of Bob Clampett and Robert McKimson have issued limited-edition cells of Tweety or Sylvester, based on original artwork from the animators themselves. Video tapes and merchandising with the pair continue to rank as top sellers, and the cat and canary are more popular today than at any other time in their careers.

Tweety and Sylvester are the classic Hollywood cartoon cat and canary. Today's animators try to imitate the cartoons of the golden age and strive to create characters with as much appeal. Tweety and Sylvester have stood the test of time and will continue to entertain generations to come.

5
FRIENDS, FOES,
AND
CO-STARS

Various friends and foes. **Above:** *Sam, the orange alley cat from "Puddy Tat Twouble" (1951).* **Below:** *Sylvester duels with Daffy in "The Scarlet Pumpernickel" (1950).*

The lesson today's animators can learn from the success and popularity of Tweety and Sylvester is that it took two strong personalities, put together as co-stars, to achieve cartoon super-stardom.

For the past five decades, Tweety and Sylvester have co-starred, separately or together, with an array of popular characters from the Warner Bros. menagerie. Some of these characters are stars in their own right, others are merely bit players, but all of them have had some hilarious moments to shine.

Elmer Fudd became befuddled at the antics of Sylvester in "Back Alley Oproar" (1948). Essentially a remake of an earlier black-and-white Porky Pig Looney Tune, "Notes to You" (1941), this cartoon features Sylvester as an alley cat who keeps Fudd awake all night with his singing from atop the backyard fence. When Elmer tries to quiet the cat by tossing a book (a copy of "The Thin Man") out the window, the cat throws the book back (now titled "Return of the Thin Man"). Sylvester pulls out all the stops when singing "Angel in Disguise" a la Spike Jones—a performance that includes dropping anvils, exploding fire crackers, and other noisy sound effects. Sylvester's other appearances with Elmer were mainly confined to comedy relief roles in a pair of semi-educational cartoons in the mid-1950s.

Sylvester has made some classic appearances with Porky Pig, each with similar themes concerning the efforts of Porky to get a good night's sleep. In "Kitty Kornered" (1946), Sylvester leads a housecat revolt against Porky, who unsuccessfully tries to put the rebellious felines out for the night. Sylvester was

Above: Title character in "Little Red Rodent Hood" (1952). *Below:* Sylvester and Porky in "Scaredy Cat" (1948). *Left:* Sylvester and Elmer Fudd in "Heir Conditioned" (1955).

recast as a more timid soul by Chuck Jones in a trilogy of Porky shorts. "Scaredy Cat" (1948) and "Claws for Alarm" (1954) place the pig and cat in various creepy gothic mansions for the night; in "Jumpin' Jupiter" (1955) a camp-out under the western skies turns into a close encounter of the third kind.

Sylvester also had a great out-of-character role in Chuck Jones's "The Scarlet Pumpernickel" (1950). In this swashbuckling spoof, which co-stars Porky Pig, Elmer Fudd, and Daffy Duck, Sylvester portrays the Grand Duke who duels with Daffy over the hand of the fair Melissa.

Some of the supporting players in the Tweety and Sylvester cartoons deserve mention. Sam, an orange tom-cat rival of Sylvester, appeared in several cartoons, each time with a differing character design. In "Puddy Tat Twouble" (1951), "Tweet and Sour" (1956), and "Trick or Tweet" (1959), Sam and Sylvester are rivals for Tweety; in "Mouse & Garden" (1960) the two square off over a little mouse.

A grumpy gray bulldog appears frequently in Sylvester cartoons, much to the cat's dismay. He is an obstacle to Tweety in such cartoons as "Fowl Weather" (1953) and "A Streetcat Named Sylvester" (1953). In "Muzzle Tough" (1954) and "Tweet and Lovely" (1959), the bulldog relentlessly pounds the pussycat in his role as the little canary's protector. The bulldog has his own special moments: as a feuding patient in the same hospital room with Tweety and Sylvester in "Greedy for Tweety" (1957), as a giant in "Tweety and the Beanstalk" (1957), as a protective daddy in "Pappy's Puppy" (1955), and as an enthusiastic devil in "Satan's Waitin'" (1954).

75

GRANNY

The old and kindly (but occasionally wacky) guardian of Tweety, Granny is often Sylvester's chief obstacle to a free canary lunch. Granny's first appearance was in 1950's "Canary Row," in which she plays an enthusiastic nemesis to Sylvester's efforts to sneak into the Broken Arms Hotel, which has a strict "No Cats and Dogs" policy.

With her spectacles and white hair tied in a bun, Granny may seem to be a harmless old lady, but to Sylvester she is to be feared. In the rare instances when Tweety can't protect himself, Granny is always there to fill in the gap, as in "Gift Wrapped," where she foils Sylvester's plans to capture Tweety with a bow and arrow—"Who were you expecting, Pocahontas?" she asks. At sea in "Tweety's S.O.S." (1951), Granny's glasses are the object of the cat's desire;

Below: An earlier version of "Granny" in Tex Avery's "Little Red Walking Hood." Right: Granny greets Sylvester for the first time in "Canary Row" (1950).

WB Limited Edition - Hand Painted

*Above: Limited edition cel by Friz Freleng. **Left:** Modified model of Granny, late 1950s.*

since she can't see him without them, Sylvester paints a crude likeness of Tweety onto one of the lenses, fooling Granny temporarily. It doesn't take long for the tables to turn, though, and when they do, she teaches him not "to molest helpless little birdies" by socking him into the sky, crashing him down onto the captain of the ocean liner.

Granny was originally voiced by actress Bea Benaderet. June Foray stepped into the role in the mid-1950s and continues to perform the role, as needed, today. Gege Pearson and Joan Gerber also voiced Granny during the 1960s.

Sylvester, Jr. in the 1950s. **Below:**
From "Too Hop to Handle"
(1956). **Bottom, right and below**
right: *Cel, model sheet, and*
animation drawing. **Opposite:**
Publicity art.

SYLVESTER Jr.

Somebody once said that you can always count on the little guys to be the instigators. Never has that been truer than in the case of Sylvester Jr.

Inquisitive and skeptical, innocent yet wise, Sylvester Jr.'s presence was both a comfort and a pain to his mouse-chasing dad Sylvester (perhaps a bit more of the latter). Created by Robert McKimson, Junior has undying pride in his pop, and his complete faith in his father's mouse-catching abilities is the catalyst for Sylvester Sr.'s disasters in many cartoons. Junior's lisping voice was, according to Bob McKimson, taken from Sylvester's.

First appearing in 1950's "Pop 'Im Pop!" Sylvester Jr. goaded his dad into chasing the giant mouse (the kangaroo Hippety Hopper). In other appearances, poppa Sylvester gets the worst of it in his efforts to fulfill his fatherly duties: failing to help his little scout earn a merit badge by chasing a vicious dwarf eagle in "The Cat's Paw" (1958), getting outsmarted by Junior's new feathered playmate in "Birds of a Father" (1961), becoming tangled up and washed out on a bungled fishing trip in "Fish and Slips" (1962), and joining the ranks of the homeless in "Claws in the Lease" (1963).

78

HIPPETY HOPPER

It's an easy mistake that anyone might make. After all, how much different does a mouse look from a kangaroo? This rather simple faux pas is capitalized on in the character Hippety Hopper. Frequently mistaken by Sylvester and Junior for a giant mouse, Hippety Hopper is actually a peaceful baby kangaroo just trying to defend himself. After having escaped from a zoo in his first appearance in "Hop, Look and Listen" (1948), Hippety hides out in Sylvester's house. The ensuing confusion leads the cat and his bulldog neighbor to literally hit the "water wagon."

The Hippety Hopper cartoons all have a similar set-up. Each time, Hippety either escapes from a nearby zoo ("Too Hop Too Handle," 1956) or circus ("Pop 'em Pop," 1950) or is innocently awaiting shipment to somewhere ("Hoppy Go Lucky," 1952). The plot usually involves Sylvester trying to prove himself

Sylvester tackles Hippety Hopper in "Too Hop to Handle" (top, 1956); "Pop 'Im Pop" (above, 1950); and "Bell Hoppy" (right, 1954).

as a master mouser to someone, most often his son. "You see, son, mice come in assorted sizes. Little ones, like the ones around here, and king-size ones, like the ones I used to hunt," brags the proud father before encountering the giant mouse. In "Bell Hoppy" (1954), a whole gang of cats ("The Loyal Order of Cats Mouse and Chowder Club") decide to grant Sylvester membership if he can put a bell around the neck of the biggest mouse he can find. The alley cats, in turn, agree to beat up on the mouse when they hear the bell ringing. Unfortunately, Hippety Hopper refuses to be belled, and Sylvester ends up getting pounced on time and time again by both Hippety and the Loyal Order.

After twelve cartoons filled with this kind of abuse, Sylvester sought professional psychiatric help in "Freudy Cat" (1964). But he, Junior, and his doctor, Dr. Freud E. Katt, run for their lives when Hippety crashes the therapy session.

*Above: Animation art. **Below:** Model sheet by Bob McKimson.*

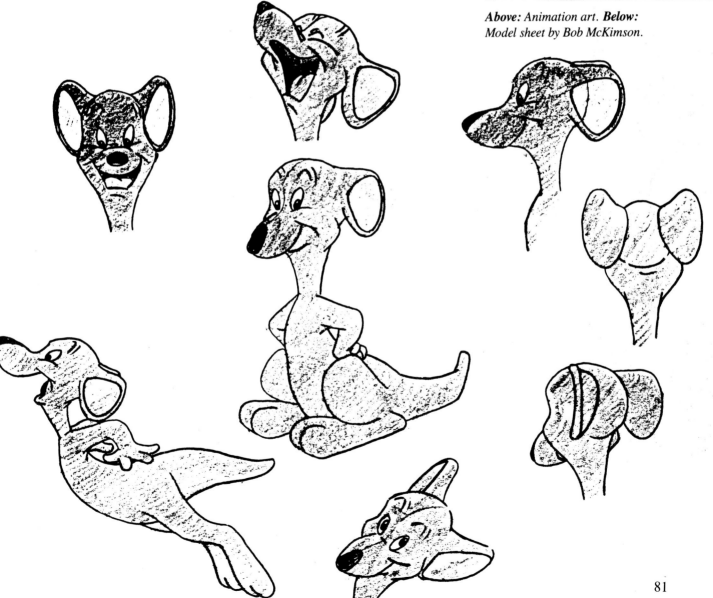

81

SPIKE AND CHESTER

If you need an animal character, and you want that character to be a typical tough-guy bully, what better choice than a bulldog? The mug, the powerful body, the angry disposition—these traits were no doubt the inspiration for Spike and Chester. Spike, a tough bulldog, and his adoring pal Chester regularly decide to beat up on cats, just for laughs. Sylvester, of course, is the unlucky victim in Friz Freleng's hilarious 1952 cartoon "Tree for Two." Luckily for the cat, a black panther escapes from the zoo, and Spike unknowingly tangles with it. Chester and Spike, you see, are under the impression that Sylvester is some kind of monster cat, the error, perhaps, of the century!

Spike and his little chatterbox sidekick Chester returned two years later in "Dr. Jerkyl's Hide." Once again, they spend their time chasing Sylvester. But this time, Sylvester has accidentally drunk some of Dr. Jekyll's infamous formula, and now it is Spike (called Alf in this film) who runs from the monstrous "Hyde-like" pussy cat.

*Below: Spike and Chester spook Sylvester in "Dr. Jerkyl's Hide" (1954). **Right:** The characters' model sheets.*

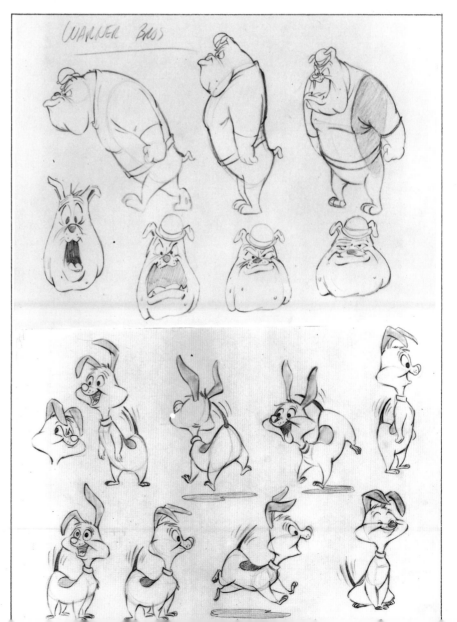

SPEEDY GONZALES

"Gringo Pussycat—eef I see you, I weel pool your tail out by eets root!"

Despite this standing threat, when Sylvester wasn't busy chasing Tweety, he tried his luck on Speedy Gonzales, the fastest mouse in all Mexico. Created by Robert McKimson in "Cat-Tails for Two" (1953), Speedy was soon redesigned and first teamed with Sylvester in Friz Freleng's 1955 Academy Award-winning cartoon "Speedy Gonzales."

Sylvester ("El gringo pussycat") is frequently thrashed by the speedy little mouse and is occasionally outsmarted by Speedy's cousin Slowpoke Rodriguez, as well. The apex of their encounters occurs in "The Wild Chase" (1965), in which Speedy races the Road Runner, with Wile E. Coyote and Sylvester in hot pursuit. The pursuant pair rig a rocket car to chase their prey, and while they don't catch either one, they do win the race!

Right: Speedy Gonzales makes good his threat to pull Sylvester's tail out "by eets roots" in "Gonzales Tamales" (1957). **Below:** *Animation sequence by Virgil Ross from "Speedy Gonzales" (1955).*

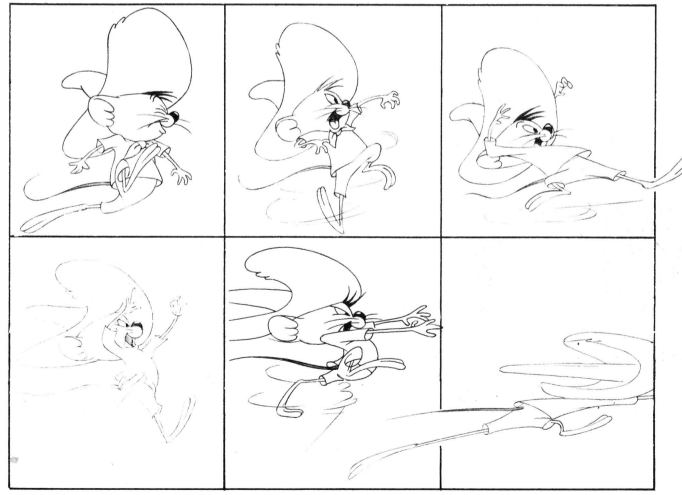

***Includes only cartoons in which he appeared with Sylvester

Filmography

1942
A TALE OF TWO KITTIES

Tweety; Babbit and Catstello; Nov 21; MM; Supervision by Robert Clampett; Story by Warren Foster; Animation by Rod Scribner. Musical Direction by Carl W. Stalling

A slicker cat, Babbit, urges his gullible partner Catstello, to "get the bird." Catstello climbs a ladder, which slowly falls apart; then he tries a large coil spring, that bounces him near a sleeping Tweety. For the very first time, Tweety "tawt he taw a puddy tat." Each time Catstello pops up, this particularly violent Tweety bird uses weapons to bat, smash, poke, squirt and dynamite him. Tweety laments, "Poor puddy tat, he cwushed his wittle head." At one point, Catstello falls on a clothesline where he hangs upside down by his toes. Tweety comes along and plays "this little piggy" until he falls. Tweety has a heart and gives the cat rope—attached to an anvil that drives him into ground. At the end of the cartoon, Catstello, propelled by a huge elastic band becomes "a spit-fire." Tweety calls for the Air Raid Warden, who orders the cat shot down. Catstello crash lands on Babbit, but they sneak up on Tweety, who shouts them back, "Turn out those lights."

1944
BIRDY AND THE BEAST

Tweety; Aug 19; MM; Directed by Robert Clampett; Story by Warren Foster; Animation by Tom McKimson; Musical Direction by Carl W. Stalling

A cat creeps along a branch toward a nest located in a tall tree. He stares, drooling, at the little bird (Tweety) sleeping inside. The bird wakes and notices the feline: "I taught I taw a putty tat." Tweety flies off the tree, and the cat follows, not realizing he is out of the tree. Tweety points that out. "The poor puddy tat! He fall down and go boom!" Tweety wanders into the cat's mouth, lights a match to see where he's going, then dons a fireman's hat and uses gasoline to douse the flames he caused. (The poor puddy tat explodes.) Eventually, the cat chases Tweety back to his nest, reaches for the bird, but gets a grenade instead, bringing on his final destruction. "You know, I lose more putty tats dat way!"

1945

LIFE WITH FEATHERS

ACADEMY
AWARD
NOMINEE

Sylvester; Mar 24; Sylvester; MM; Directed by I. Freleng; Story by Tedd Pierce; Animation by Virgil Ross; Musical Direction by Carl W. Stalling

A love bird has a major fight with his wife and decides to end it all by letting a cat eat him. Sylvester finds the bird and shouts "Sufferin' succotash! Squab." But Sylvester becomes suspicious at the bird's willingness and refuses to eat him. The bird tries to get into Sylvester's mouth, malleting his foot and flying into it when he screams, tempting him with food images. When Sylvester finally gives in, the bird receives a telegram from his wife telling him that all is forgiven, and the tables turn, with Sylvester chasing the bird—until the end of the cartoon when the wife comes home and the bird chases Sylvester once again.

Above, and following right-hand pages: Sylvester tries to sneak up on Speedy Gonzales and ends up blasting into space in this animation sequence by Virgil Ross from "Mexican Cat Dance" (1962). These animation drawings have been arranged as a flip book.

A GRUESOME TWOSOME

Tweety; June 9; MM; Directed by Bob Clampett; Story by Warren Foster; Animation by Robert McKimson, Manny Gould, Basil Davidovich, and Rod Scribner; Layouts and Backgrounds by Thomas McKimson and Michael Sasanoff; Effects Animation by A.C. Gamer; Voice Characterization by Mel Blanc; Musical Direction by Carl W. Stalling

Two cats (one a caricature of Jimmy Durante, the other a dumb, potbellied goof) are rivals for a sexy female feline who tells them, "Whoever brings me a little bird can be my fella." They both sneak up on the "naked genius," Tweety who beats them with a sledgehammer, sending them crashing to the ground ("Aw! The poor putty tats! They faw down and go boom!").

The cats team up disguised as a horse (in history's phoniest pony suit). Tweety pulls a bumblebee out of his pants, slaps it around, and shoves it into the horse costume. This creates a bucking bronco that Tweety rides like the Lone Ranger. Tweety then steals a bone from a vicious bulldog and throws it into the horse suit, leading the dog to destroy the cats once and for all. Says Tweety, "I get wid of more putty tats dat way!"

Peck Up Your Troubles

PECK UP YOUR TROUBLES

Sylvester; Oct 20; MM; Directed by I. Freleng; Story by Michael Maltese; Animation by Ken Champin; Musical Direction by Carl Stalling

A hungry Sylvester chases a silent, little woodpecker. He tries stilts but the woodpecker pecks them apart, leaving him hanging on a branch until the bird pecks out a dotted line and then cuts along it. Sylvester then tries tightrope walking on the electric wires, but gets zapped. The bird tricks Sylvester into thinking he's crushed him, dresses as an angel, and suggests suicide to assuage a guilty conscience, but Sylvester sees through the plot. After a few more attempts to get the bird, Sylvester decides to dynamite the tree, but a bulldog changes his mind. The woodpecker causes the dynamite to explode around Sylvester, who ends up on a cloud in a real angel outfit.

1946
KITTY KORNERED

Porky Pig, Sylvester; June 8; LT; Directed by Robert Clampett; Animation by Manny Gould, Rod Scribner, and C. Melendez; Layouts and Backgrounds by Thomas McKimson and Dorcy Howard; Voice Characterization by Mel Blanc; Musical Direction by Carl W. Stalling

At Porky Pig's house, the cats throw *him* out. Inside, four pussycats are drinking "Arsenic and Old Grapes" and singing "Auld Lang Syne." Porky makes a startling appearance at the window, and the cats scram. Porky pulls one cat from a hanging moose head, extracting the moose himself from the wall! Porky threatens the cats with his dog Lassie (Porky using hand-shadows). This sends three of the cats out the front door and one down the kitchen drain. Sylvester speaks: "Brother pussycats! We've been skidded out, scooted out, backed out, and booted out! It's un-catstitutional!" They dress as Martians and wake Porky with a frantic news report about "Men from Mars landing on Earth." Porky panics when he sees Martians around his bed and runs for his musket. The cats charge Porky a la Teddy Roosevelt's Rough Riders. Porky lands in the snow and asks, "Does anyone in the audience know somebody who has a house to rent?"

1947

TWEETIE PIE

ACADEMY AWARD WINNER

Tweety, Sylvester; May 3; MM; Directed by I. Freleng.

Warner Bros.' first Oscar-winning cartoon, and the first pairing of Tweety and Sylvester. While Tweety warms himself in the snow near a cigar butt, Sylvester (called Thomas in this picture) sneaks up and makes a grab for him. Sylvester's master finds Tweety wrapped in his tail, takes the bird inside, puts it in a birdcage, and warns Thomas not to try any tricks.

Sylvester tries piling up the furniture to reach the birdcage, but Tweety saws a chair leg, causing a crash. When the cat next tries metal furniture, Tweety uses a blowtorch. Sylvester uses an electric fan to fly to the cage, but Tweety pulls the plug. Sylvester's fishing-rod pulley doesn't work. The cat catches Tweety under a glass, but a pin point makes Sylvester scream, bringing the lady of the house, who throws the cat out. When he saws a hole in the ceiling around the birdcage, the attic drops into the living room. In the end, Sylvester gets hit with a shovel by his new master, Tweety!

CROWING PAINS

Foghorn Leghorn, Sylvester, Henery Hawk; July 12; LT; Directed by Robert McKimson; Story by Warren Foster; Animation by John Carey, I. Ellis, Charles McKinson, and Manny Gould; Layouts by Cornett Wood; Backgrounds by Richard H. Thomas; Voice Characterization by Mel Blanc; Musical Direction by Carl W. Stalling

A bush moves around the barnyard. It's Sylvester trying to steal the barnyard dog's bone. The dog chases the cat, but his rope restrains and chokes him. Sylvester tries to hit the dog with an axe, but Foghorn Leghorn grabs the weapon, ordering the cat to "bury the hatchet!" Meanwhile, Henery Hawk grabs Foghorn and drags him away. Foggy instructs Henery that a chicken has black fur like Sylvester's, puts Henery in a trick egg and places it underneath the cat. Henery, inside the egg, tries to stick with Sylvester and chases him around the barnyard. Sylvester tries to tell Henery he's not a chicken, but that Foghorn is. They argue and soon the dog joins in. Henery decides to wait till dawn to see who crows. At dawn, the crowing emanates from Sylvester, and Henery drags him away. Foghorn, with a ventriloquism manual in hand, advises, "I say you gotta keep on your toes."

DOGGONE CATS

Sylvester; Oct 25; MM; Directed by Arthur Davis; Story by Lloyd Turner and Bill Scott; Animation by Basil Davidovich, J.C. Melendez, Don Williams, and Emery Hawkins; Layouts by Don Smith; Backgrounds by Philip DeGuard

A goofy Sylvester and his orange feline friend are chased by Wellington the bulldog, who has been given strict orders by his lady master to deliver a package to Uncle Louie. The two cats pester the dog all along the way, eventually getting the package from him. Wellington chases the cats, who disguise a weight as the parcel and toss the phoney package off a bridge. Wellington goes after it in a boat that smashes and sinks. Wellington next gets run over by a steamroller while trying protect the package. Battered and beat, Wellington finally delivers the parcel to Uncle Louie which turns out to contain dinner for the two cats!

CATCH AS CATS CAN

Sylvester; Dec 6; MM; Directed by Arthur Davis; Story by Dave Monahan; Animation by J.C. Melendez, Basil Davidovich, Don Williams, and Herman Cohen; Layouts by Don Smith; Backgrounds by Philip DeGuard; Effects Animation by A.C. Gamer; Voice Characterization by Mel Blanc; Musical Direction by Carl W. Stalling

A jealous Crosby parrot conspires with a hungry Sylvester to kill a Sinatra canary. One of their schemes involves Crosby giving Sylvester a knife and a bar of soap that he carves into a beautiful girl canary decoy. It is placed near a greased kitchen counter. The canary sends the soap decoy sliding into the cat's mouth. Finally, Sylvester dresses as a maid, and vacuums up the bird. The canary turns the tables by tying the cat's tail to the vacuum handle, his mouth to the pipe. The cat proceeds to suck up everything in the house, including the hot coals in the fireplace. In the end, Sylvester has eaten the parrot and has assumed the Crosby mannerisms with pipe and hat!

1948
BACK ALLEY OPROAR

Elmer Fudd; Sylvester; Mar 27; MM; Directed by I. Freleng; Story by Michael Maltese and Tedd Pierce; Animation by Gerry Chiniquy, Manuel Perez, Ken Champin, and Virgil Ross; Layouts by Hawley Pratt; Backgrounds by Paul Julian; Voice Characterization by Mel Blanc; Musical Direction by Carl W. Stalling

A color remake of "Notes to You" (1941). Just as a sleepy Elmer Fudd gets in bed, Sylvester sets up his music stand on the backyard fence. When Sylvester sings "Figaro," Elmer throws a pair of old shoes at him. Sylvester uses the shoes to stomp out the "Second Hungarian Rhapsody," up the porch steps. Singing "Some Sunday Morning," Elmer throws a book ("The Thin Man"), which the cat throws back (as "Return of the Thin Man"). Elmer runs outside to chase the cat. Sylvester has lined the steps with grease and tacks. The cat sings "You Never Know Where You're Going Till You Get There," sees Elmer coming, and hands his sheet music to a big dumb orange cat, who goes into a soprano opera solo until Elmer crowns him. Elmer corners Sylvester, but the pussycat lulls Fudd to sleep by singing "Go to Sleep." Getting Fudd back into bed, Sylvester wakes him again by becoming a one-man band. Elmer lights a box of dynamite, which explodes, sending him to peaceful heaven to be joined by Sylvester's musical nine lives!

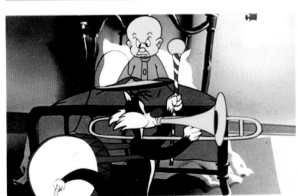

I TAW A PUTTY TAT

Tweety, Sylvester; Apr 2; MM; Directed by I. Freleng; Story by Tedd Pierce; Animation by Virgil Ross, Gerry Chiniquy, Manuel Perez, and Ken Chapin; Layouts by Hawley Pratt; Backgrounds by Paul Julian; Voice Characterization by Mel Blanc; Musical Direction by Carl W. Stalling. In Cinecolor.

A semi-remake of Tashlin's "Puss N' Booty" (1943), right down to the same street address, 1605 Maple Drive, starring Tweety and Sylvester in the leading cat and canary roles. Sylvester awaits the arrival of a new canary, Tweety. Sylvester asks the bird to stand still, and, when he does, he puts him in his mouth. Tweety lights a match to see what's going on, and in the smoke he flies out. The bird mallets the cat's paw to retrieve his "widdle hat." They play tag, and Sylvester reaches for the bird on the pantry shelf. Tweety accidently has eaten some alum and Sylvester is able to suck him into his mouth via a straw. Inside, Tweety works out, using the cat's tonsils as a punching bag. While playing hide and seek, Sylvester hits a vicious "puddy dog" with a mallet, leading the dog to him. Tweety brings both pets together in his birdcage. In the end, the lady of the house calls the pet shop to order a new cat.

HOP LOOK AND LISTEN

Sylvester, Hippety Hopper; Apr 17; LT; Directed by Robert McKimson; Story by Warren Foster; Animation by Charles McKimson, Manny Gould, and I. Ellis; Layouts by Cornett Wood; Backgrounds by Richard Thomas; Voice Characterizations by Mel Blanc.

In this first of a long series of Hippety Hopper cartoons, a baby kangaroo hops out of his cage to explore the neighborhood. He finds Sylvester "fishing" for mice and throwing back some that are too small. Sylvester mistakes Hippety for a giant mouse. He runs aways but his bulldog friend laughs at him for being afraid of a mouse. Hippety trounces Sylvester soundly until his mother comes to claim him—at which point the bulldog and Sylvester both leave on the water wagon.

KIT FOR CAT

Sylvester, Elmer Fudd; Nov 6; LT; Directed by I. Freleng; Story by Michael Maltese and Tedd Pierce; Animation by Virgil Ross, Gerry Chiniquy, Manuel Perez, and Ken Chapin; Layouts by Hawley Pratt; Backgrounds by Paul Julian; Voice Characterization by Mel Blanc; Musical Direction by Carl W. Stalling

Kit for Cat

Homeless alley cat Sylvester and an orange kitten vie for leftovers in the trash cans. Both end up in the home of Elmer Fudd, who says he would like to keep one of the cats, but not both. Sylvester plans to do in his kitten companion. While Fudd sleeps on his decision, Sylvester tries to frame the little feline by breaking milk bottles and a dozen dishes in the kitchen and hypnotizing the kitten to bat Fudd over the head. Each plan gets Sylvester in more trouble. After several noisy interludes, Fudd's landlord evicts him, and all three go back to the alley.

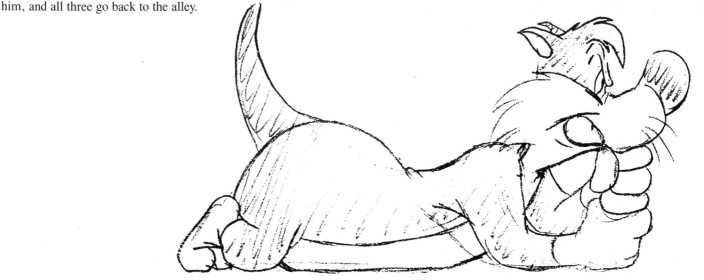

Hop, Look and Listen

SCAREDY CAT

Porky Pig, Sylvester; Dec 18; MM; Directed by Charles M. Jones; Story by Michael Maltese; Animation by Lloyd Vaughan, Ken Harris, Phil Monroe, and Ben Washam; Layouts by Robert Gribbroek; Backgrounds by Peter Alvarado; Voice Characterization by Mel Blanc; Musical Direction by Carl W. Stalling

On a dark night, Porky Pig brings Sylvester to their new home, a gothic mansion. Sylvester is scared out of his wits and clings to Porky at every moment. As he goes up to bed, Porky orders the cat into the kitchen, but Sylvester sticks so close to Porky that the pig puts his bed clothes on around the cat. Porky throws the coward out. Downstairs, Sylvester sees a death march, black-hooded mice wheeling a cat to execution. Sylvester runs back to Porky, but the pig orders him out. Sylvester grabs a gun and threatens to kill himself. With that, Porky lets him stay.

Sylvester has a night of horror, while the only thing disturbing Porky is the cat's cowardice. The mice throw Porky's bed out the window; drop an anvil on the pig; attempt to kill both with knives, trapdoors, arrows, bowling balls, and so on. Only Sylvester is aware of what's happening. Porky drags the pussycat to the kitchen to prove what "a yellow dog of a cowardly cat" he is. In the kitchen, Porky is bound and gagged and wheeled off to execution, with a sign, "You were right, Sylvester!" The cat runs from the house, but his conscience reminds him of how Porky raised him. The cat grabs a tree trunk and beats off the mice, saving Porky and earning his respect once again.

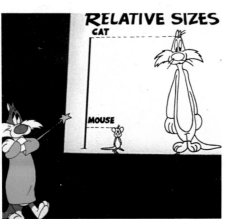

1949
MOUSE MAZURKA

Sylvester; June 11; MM; Directed by I. Freleng; Story by Tedd Pierce; Animation by Gerry Chiniquy, Ken Champin, Virgil Ross, and Manuel Perez; Backgrounds by Paul Julian; Layouts by Hawley Pratt; Voice Characterization by Mel Blanc; Musical Direction by Carl W. Stalling

In the Slobovian Mountains, Boris Borscht, the Bagel Baron, has his home, and in it lives a mouse with a red village hat who polka-dances while he steals food. Enter Sylvester, with a green village hat, who intends to catch the mouse. While the mouse is out of his hole, Sylvester changes the lock on his door. The mouse mallets the cat, and the key is ejected on his tongue. Next, Sylvester disguises his hand as a Slobovian village girl. The mouse dances with the girl and then brings her into his mouse hole and disguises the "girl" as a mouse. Sylvester mallets his own fingers. Sylvester chases the mouse behind some bottles, and the mouse pretends to be tossing a vial of nitroglycerine. The mouse accidentally (and unknowingly) drinks some real nitro and tortures Sylvester as he jumps off the cabinet, smokes, and dives off the rafters, confident

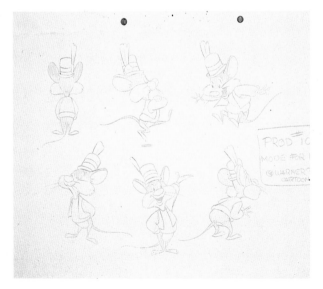

that Sylvester will catch him. Sylvester takes the whole weight of a falling safe on his shoulders. The mouse does a violent jig, but his jig is up! He explodes and floats to heaven. The narrator laughs at Sylvester, saying, "Now you'll never catch that mouse." Sylvester responds, "That's what you think!" He drinks some nitro, explodes, and chases the mouse into heavenly clouds.

BAD OL' PUTTY TAT

Tweety, Sylvester; July 23; Directed by Friz Freleng; Story by Tedd Pierce; Animation by Gerry Chiniquy, Manuel Perez, Ken Champin, and Virgil Ross; Backgrounds by Paul Julian; Layouts by Hawley Pratt; Voice Characterization by Mel Blanc; Musical Direction by Carl W. Stalling

The film begins with a pan downward on Tweety's barb-wired birdhouse, with a ruffled Sylvester below, plotting his next move. The cat uses a girdle to bounce up to the birdhouse, but each time he jumps up Tweety pushes something in his face. Finally, the little bird shoves a stick of dynamite in the cat's diving helmet. Tweety escapes the birdhouse by sliding down a clothes wire. The wire is attached to the cat's tooth and Tweety attaches his end of the wire to a sky-rocket, which blasts the cat's teeth out of his head. Sylvester disguises his finger as a girl canary in a nest. As Tweety comes to her, Sylvester catches Tweety with his hand. Tweety switches his hat for "her" bonnet, and the cat bites his own finger. Tweety hides near a badminton game, becoming the "birdie." Sylvester joins the game, intending to catch Tweety with his mouth. Tweety drops a lit stick of dynamite instead. Trying to put out the fuse, the cat winds up inside the watercooler. In an act of desperation, Sylvester disguises his head to look like Tweety's birdhouse. Tweety enters, but takes control of the cat, imitating a railroad locomotive. Tweety, with an appropriate engineer's cap, steers the putty tat into a brick wall. "You know, I lose more putty tats dat way!"

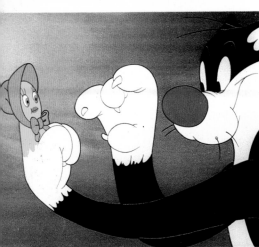

HIPPETY HOPPER

Sylvester, Hippety Hopper; Nov 19; MM; Directed by Robert McKimson; Story by Warren Foster; Animation by Pete Burness, John Carey, Charles McKimson, and Phil DeLara; Layouts by Cornett Wood; Backgrounds by Richard H. Thomas; Voice Characterization by Mel Blanc; Musical Direction by Carl W. Stalling

At the waterfront, a mouse about to commit suicide is saved by a kangaroo, Hippety Hopper, awaiting delivery to the city zoo. The mouse enlists Hippety's aid in getting even with the cat, Sylvester. The mouse tells Sylvester he will "take vitamins and grow as big as you are!" Sylvester laughs until he sees Hippety, who boxes him into the wall and tosses him out of the house. A bulldog sends the confused cat back in. Hippety punches him out again. Sylvester tells the dog that the mouse is a giant. The dog puts a pair of glasses on the cat and assures him, "Nobody hits a guy with glasses. Of course, I could be wrong!" After Sylvester comes crashing out again, the bulldog goes in and dares the mouse to kick him out. Hippety kicks, the mouse bites, and the dog goes running. The mouse threatens to pin the dog's ears back. The dog replies, "Any time a mouse can pin my ears back, I'll take ballet lessons!" The film ends with Sylvester and the bulldog pirouetting into the sunset.

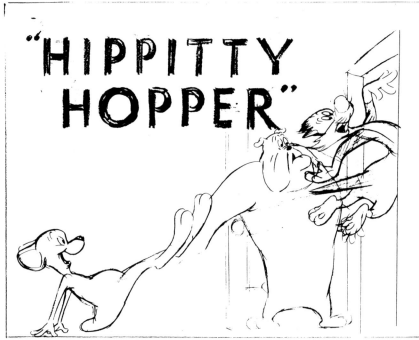

1950
HOME TWEET HOME

Tweety, Sylvester; Jan 14; MM; Directed by I. Freleng; Story by Tedd Piece; Animation by Virgil Ross, Arthur Davis, Gerry Chiniquy, and Ken Champin; Layouts by Hawley Pratt; Backgrounds by Phil DeLara; Voice Characterization by Mel Blanc; Musical Direction by Carl W. Stalling

Tweety is taking a bath in the park birdbath. Sylvester sneaks closer, pretending to read the paper on the park bench. The cat gets so close that Tweety uses his tongue as a towel to dry off. As the cat chases the bird around a park statue, a nanny comes to Tweety's rescue, beating the cat away. ("You coward, you bully, you shmo!") Sylvester disguises himself as the nanny's charge and complains, "Baby wants a pretty birdie!" When the nanny gives him Tweety, he puts the bird right in his mouth, for which the nanny spanks him. Tweety escapes to a window ledge.

    Sylvester follows, using bubblegum to float upward. Tweety pops his gum and hands him an anvil (then "saves" the cat with an anvil-stuffed pillow!). Sylvester disguises himself as a tree. A bulldog falling for the disguise, sniffs him and chases him. Tweety calls the pet shop to order another putty tat. "I'm fwesh out!"

Home Tweet Home

100

THE SCARLET PUMPERNICKEL

Daffy Duck and a cast of thousands; Mar 4; LT; Directed by Charles M. Jones;
Story by Michael Maltese; Animation by Phil Monroe, Ben Washam, Lloyd Vaughan,
and Ken Harris; Layouts by Robert Gribbroek; Backgrounds by Peter Alvarado;
Voice Characterization by Mel Blanc; Musical Direction by Carl W. Stalling

"You're killing me," screams Daffy.   Pleading for a dramatic part with a studio big-
wig, Daffy Duck produces a script about a swashbuckling highwayman, (Daffy as Errol
Flynn) a Lord High Chamberlain (Porky Pig as Claude Rains) and Milady
Melissa. To set a trap for "That masked stinker," the Chamberlain announces the betrothal
of Melissa to the Grand Duke (Sylvester as Basil Rathbone). The Pumpernickel stops
at the King's Nostril Inn, run by Elmer Fudd (Blanc not Bryan), masquerading as a
foppish gentleman, his disguise fooling the Chamberlain and the Duke. After a few
slapstick pratfalls, Daffy crashes the wedding (literally) and rescues his lady love from
the very threshold of the altar; the whole thing climaxes in a swordfight, that, as the
studio boss begs for the finish, is only the first of a series of climaxes that includes the
cavalry, bursting dams, erupting volcanos, and skyrocketing prices of kosher food.

ALL A-BIR-R-R-D

Tweety, Sylvester; June 24; LT; Directed by I. Freleng; Story by Tedd Pierce;
Animation by Ken Champin, Virgil Ross, Arthur Davis, Emery Hawkins, and
Gerry Chiniquy; Backgrounds by Paul Julian; Layouts by Hawley Pratt; Voice
Characterization by Mel Blanc; Musical Direction by Carl W. Stalling

The Scarlet Pumpernickel

"Mommy" (voiced by Bea Benederet) puts Tweety alone on a train bound for Gower
Gulch. Tweety sings his little song ("I'm a tweet little bird in a gilded cage/Tweety's
my name, but I don't know my age..."), attracting that hungry putty tat, Sylvester. The
conductor warns the cat off and puts Tweety's cage on a higher perch. That doesn't
stop the cat from trying. Sylvester stacks baggage and climbs for the bird. Tweety pulls
the emergency brake and sends the cat into the furnace! Sylvester angers a large bulldog, also riding in the car. Sylvester grabs Tweety, but the conductor comes by, so the
cat stashes the bird in the mail sack and hangs it on the mail hook. Sylvester runs to
retrieve his dinner, opens the mail sack, and is surprised by the dog. The dog chases
the cat atop the train, and Sylvester falls off. At the Gower Gulch station, a lady (Sylvester
in disguise) picks up Tweety, but gets the dog instead, who pummels the puss!

CANARY ROW

Tweety, Sylvester; Oct 7; LT; Directed by I. Freleng; Story by Tedd Pierce; Animation by Virgil Ross, Arthur Davis, Emery Hawkings, Gerry Chiniquy, and Ken Champin; Layouts by Hawley Pratt; Backgrounds by Paul Julian; Voice Characterization by Mel Blanc; Musical Direction by Carl W. Stalling

In the headquarters of the Bird Watcher's Society, Sylvester spies through his binoculars at Tweety in the window of the Broken Arms Hotel. Since dogs and cats are not allowed in the place, Sylvester is summarily bounced from the lobby, and when he climbs up the drainpipe he is heaved out the window (down a couple of stories) by Granny. When Granny calls down to the desk clerk for a boy to carry her bags, Sylvester comes and successfully sneaks out with the cage only to find Granny waiting for him with an umbrella. Lastly, he tightrope walks atop cable-car wires and ends up fleeing electro-

cution from a trolley that turns out to be engineered by Tweety and Granny ("You did see a puddy tat!").

STOOGE FOR A MOUSE

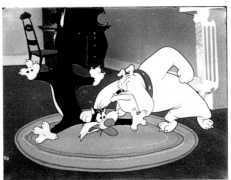

Sylvester; Oct 21; MM; Directed by I. Freleng; Animation by Arthur Davis, Gerry Chiniquy, Emery Hawkins, Ken Chapin, and Virgil Ross; Layouts by Hawley Pratt; Backgrounds by Paul Julian; Voice Characterization by Mel Blanc; Musical Direction by Carl W. Stalling

Sylvester is resting comfortably on his friend Mike the bulldog. A mouse sneaks out of his hole and tries to get some cheese, but Sylvester traps him in his mouth. The mouse escapes back to his hole, saws a hole in the ceiling, and lowers a telephone toward the dog's ear. He tells the dog, "All the dogs in the alley are talking about you. They say you are a sissy, that you like cats. How come?" The mouse plants a knife in Sylvester's hand and tells Mike, "He's gonna cut your throat!" The dog wakes the confused cat and orders him to the other side of the room. The mouse eventually ruins the friendship of the cat and the dog and a battle ensues. They wreck the house and knock themselves out. The mouse now walks out to get his cheese.

POP 'IM POP!

Sylvester, Hippety Hopper; Oct 28; LT; Directed by Robert McKimson; Story by Warren Foster; Animation by Charles McKimson, Rod Scribner, Phil DeLara, Manuel Perez, and J.C. Melendez; Layouts by Cornett Wood; Backgrounds by Richard H. Thomas; Voice Characterization by Mel Blanc; Musical Direction by Carl W. Stalling

At the circus, the show barker introduces Gracie, the Fighting Kangaroo, and her son, Hippety Hopper, who bounces out of the circus and down the street, ruining a cement worker's freshly laid sidewalk (a running gag). Meanwhile, Sylvester is telling his son tall tales about catching a giant mouse. When Hippety comes behind him, Junior goads his dad into fighting the giant rodent. "C'mon, Pop! Go get the mouse like you said you could, unless you want to destroy a child's faith in his father!" Sylvester boxes with the kangaroo in the yard, getting beaten to a pulp. Sylvester chases the "giant mouse" down the street into the fresh cement and into the circus tent. Just as Sylvester is boasting to his son about beating the mouse, "Why, I wish he was twice as big, with two heads and four arms. . . ." Gracie, with Hippety in her pouch, emerges from the circus tent, scaring the cats away.

1951

CANNED FEUD

Sylvester; Feb 3; LT; Directed by I. Freleng; Story by Warren Foster and Cal Howard; Animation by Ken Champin, Virgil Ross, Arthur Davis, Manuel Perez, and John Carey; Backgrounds by Paul Julian; Layouts by Hawley Pratt; Voice Characterization by Mel Blanc; Musical Direction by Carl W. Stalling

This cartoon is Freleng's masterpiece of timing, pantomime, and the lost art of building and releasing tension. Instead of having Sylvester's angst slowly gather momentum, it begins with the cat totally freaking out when he realizes that his people have gone on vacation and forgotten to put him out. Sylvester discovers a pantry full of canned goods, but the only can opener is to be found in the hands of a wise guy mouse who taunts the out-of-control cat into smashing into walls, electrocuting himself, and dropping a piano on his own head. The tension is enough to make you sweat. Finally—after trying to open the can with an axe and getting sucked into a vacuum—Sylvester gets the can opener. And the mouse has put a lock on the pantry door—and holds the only key.

PUDDY TAT TWOUBLE

Tweety, Sylvester; Feb 24; LT; Directed by I. Freleng; Story by Warren Foster; Animation by Arthur Davis, Manuel Perez, Ken Champin, and Virgil Ross; Layouts by Hawley Pratt; Backgrounds by Paul Julian; Voice Characterization by Mel Blanc; Musical Direction by Carl W. Stalling

"This is what I get for dweaming of a white Chwistmas," says Tweety, shoveling snow out of his nest atop a pole. He's been spotted by Sylvester on one side and a big orange tabby on the other ("Hey! I'm suwwounded by puddy tats!"). Both chase the bird, beating each other up along the way (but without dialogue; the cats are silent, all the lines going to Tweety). Having grabbed the bird, they zip back and forth between their two buildings until Sylvester falls into a cellar. There, Tweety chances upon a toy "dunking bird" and mistakes it for a real bird ("What's the matter? Puddy tat got your tongue?"). The orange cat does the same and swallows the dunker, thinking it's Tweety, and is compelled to perform the dunking motion. When Tweety hides in Sylvester's mouth, the orange cat snatches him out and runs back upstairs with Sylvester hurling heavy objects at him but missing. Orange sticks his tongue out at Sylvester, gets kay-

oed by an iron, and slides down the stairs holding Tweety ("Let's do dat again, dat was fun!"). After Tweety's dodging into a section of pipe leads to more cat battling, Tweety runs back out into the snow and tricks the cats into running over a frozen lake, where he ice-picks out a hole around them. We end on both puddies suffering colds in their respective domiciles. "Da poor puddy tats."

ROOM AND BIRD

Tweety, Sylvester; June 2; MM; Directed by I. Freleng; Story by Tedd Pierce, Warren Foster; Animation by Virgil Ross, Arthur Davis, Manuel Perez, and Ken Champin; Layouts by Hawley Pratt; Backgrounds by Paul Julian; Voice Characterizations by Mel Blanc; Musical Direction by Eugene Poddany; Orchestrations by Milt Franklyn

At the Spinsters Arms Hotel (subtitled "Baby, It's Cold Inside"), a tough-looking dick is on hand to enforce the no-pets-allowed rule. Tweety and Sylvester are snuck in by their mistresses (who aren't heard from again). Hearing Tweety sing ("I'm a tweety wittle bird"), Sylvester writes him a letter: "I'm just mad about your singing. Come over and we'll make beautiful music together." The familiar cat-and-bird (and later dog) antics are periodically interrupted by the suspicious detective, so the animals take care to whoosh quietly by him. Sylvester tries climbing furniture, then taking the place of an elevator, which Tweety unwittingly descends. Sylvester learns rather late in the next scene that he's been walking on a bulldog's head. Bird, cat, and dog turn up running out of every door but the one the detective is facing. Ultimately, he broadcasts, "Attention, everyone! Someone has pets in this house, and I want them out of here imme-

diately." He's immediately caught in the middle of a stampede of domestic and wild animals, about which he utters his own, "I tawt I taw" line, to which Tweety adds, "You did see a puddy tat, a moo-moo cow, a big gorilla, a diddyap horsie, and a wittle monkey."

TWEETY'S SOS

Tweety, Sylvester; Sept 22; MM; Directed by I. Freleng; Story by Warren Foster; Animation by Arthur Davis, Manuel Perez, Ken Champin, and Virgil Ross; Layouts by Hawley Pratt; Backgrounds by Paul Julian; Voice Characterization by Mel Blanc; Musical Direction by Carl W. Stalling

Starving Sylvester, despondent on a dockside, spies Tweety through an ocean liner porthole and purrs, "Hello, breakfast!" Nearsighted Granny is also aboard, and she'll teach him "to molest helpless little birdies." Granny's glasses are important: if Sylvester can keep them away from her, he can get at the bird. Tweety's restoring them to Granny's face keeps Sylvester away. The cat paints crude Tweety images on both lenses so they form a cel and background Tweety when she looks at his cage, giving him time to chase the bird. When Tweety sees that the seasick cat is turning green, he offers him a "nice fat juicy piece of salt pork." Sylvester downs some seasick remedy and gives chase once again, dashing into the furnace by mistake.

Tweety rekindles his seasickness by rocking a picture of a boat. This time Sylvester swallows nitroglycerine, which bestows on him the desirable cartoon power of explosive expectorations. Granny clobbers him with her umbrella and sends him into orbit. He lands on the captain, who thinks he saw a puddy tat. At the helm, Granny and Tweety confirm in unison, "You did, you did see a puddy tat!"

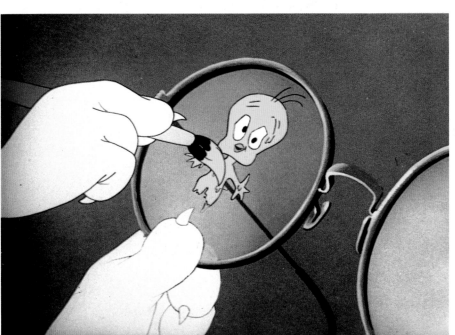

TWEET, TWEET TWEETY

Tweety, Sylvester; Dec 15; LT; Directed by I. Freleng; Story by Warren Foster; Animation by Manuel Perez, Ken Champin, Virgil Ross, and Arthur Davis; Layouts by Hawley Pratt; Backgrounds by Paul Julian; Effects Animation by Harry Love; Voice Characterization by Mel Blanc; Musical Direction by Carl W. Stalling

Sylvester's owners camp in a national forest, and the cat immediately makes for a nest he has spied atop a tree, despite the game warden's warning that hunting and fishing are not permitted in this game refuge. He finds an egg in the nest, and it hatches, giving birth to Tweety, who says, "Get that catty carcass off me" and does with the aid of a pin. Sylvester tries pumping Tweety out of the tree with an air pump, then tries chopping the enormous tree down and swinging up to him. He gets flattened in both attempts. When Tweety poses proudly before amateur wildlife photographers, Sylvester sneaks up on him with a phony tripod. Finally, Sylvester, in a rowboat, chases Tweety

down a river that leads to a waterfall, but he doesn't notice until he's rowed much too far. Tweety shouts, "Keep wowing, puddy tat, I'll save you!" and then turns a dial that blocks off the water.

1952
WHO'S KITTEN WHO

Jan 5; LT; Directed by Robert McKimson; Story by Tedd Pierce; Animation by Phil DeLara, Emery Hawkins, Charles McKimson, and Rod Scribner; Layouts by Peter Alvarado; Backgrounds by Richard H. Thomas; Voice Characterization by Mel Blanc; Musical Direction by Carl W. Stalling

Hippety Hopper, inside a crate headed for the zoo, hops off and enters the basement of a house just as Sylvester is lecturing his wee one on "The mysteries of life." (mouse-catching), boasting, "I'm the cat who can show you all the tricks of the trade. They don't come tricky enough or big enough for your father." Or do they? Hippety Hopper repeatedly bounces Sylvester out of the room to the shame of his boy. "Wherever I go," Junior laments, "people will point at me and say, 'There goes the kid whose father was thrown out by a mouse!' "

GIFT WRAPPED

Tweety, Sylvester; Feb 16; LT; Directed by I. Freleng; Story by Warren Foster;
Animation by Arthur Davis, Manuel Perez, Ken Champin, and Virgil Ross; Layouts
by Hawley Pratt; Backgrounds by Irv Wyner; Voice Characterization by Mel Blanc;
Musical Direction by Carl W. Stalling

On the night before Christmas, Sylvester is upset over the absence of mice ("not a
creature was stirring, not even—"). Morning brings him excitement: "Oh, goody, goody!
Santa Claus came for real! Oh, I've been a good pussycat!" He's disappointed when
he gets a rubber mouse instead of a real one and shows more interest in Granny's gift:
Tweety in a cage. He switches the gift labels and eats Tweety, but Granny makes him
spit Tweety out. As soon as Granny has gone, Sylvester's at the bird again, briefly

distracted by a big unopened box under the tree that contains a huge bulldog. Cat chases
bird and dog chases cat until Granny tapes up their mouths with Christmas seals and
has them all sing "Hark the Herald Angels."

LITTLE RED RODENT HOOD

Sylvester; May 3; MM; Directed by I. Freleng; Story by Warren Foster; Animation
by Ken Champin, Virgil Ross, Arthur Davis, and Manuel Perez; Layouts by Hawley
Pratt; Backgrounds by Irv Wyner; Voice Characterization by Mel Blanc; Musical
Direction by Carl W. Stalling

Sweet little Timmy mouse visualizes the story of Red Riding Hood in cat-and-mouse
terms, with a mousified Granny telling him the tale. and Sylvester as the big bad wolf,
who, in grandma drag, ejects three other similarly clad would-be bad pussycats who
want to get in on the act. Timmy goes through the familiar dialogue with Sylvester and
they all get in trouble with a bulldog and dynamite. Sylvester poses as the tyke's "Fairy
Godmother," complete with an electric cattle-prod magic wand that the dog tricks him
into using on himself. After blowing Sylvester up with a toy tank, Timmy holes up.
End of story, almost. "Luckily, Little Red Riding Hood found a large firecracker left
over from the Fourth of July." Says the mouse, "I bet that blew him all up." Says Sylvester,
"You're not just whistling 'Dixie,' brother."

AIN'T SHE TWEET

Tweety, Sylvester; June 21; LT; Directed by I. Freleng; Story by Warren Foster; Animation by Virgil Foster, Arthur Davis, Manuel Perez, and Ken Champin; Layouts by Hawley Pratt; Backgrounds by Irv Wyner; Voice Characterization by Mel Blanc; Musical Direction by Carl W. Stalling

Sylvester and Tweety encounter each other on opposite sides of a pet shop window. Tweety is taken to Granny, the daffy old dame who's wild about pets and, Sylvester is not too thrilled to learn, keeps a yard full of frisky bulldogs. Sylvester tries to get up to the second story window where Tweety is caged by walking across a branch (which Tweety saws off) and by using stilts (which are demolished by the dogs after Tweety gives them tools). Then he builds a rocket from a blueprint but only sets his fur on fire. He waits until the doggies have left the yard but finds them in the house (an old man, thinking he's doing Sylvester a favor, shoves him back over the fence). He hides in a package he thinks is intended for Granny, but it actually contains dog food. Lastly, he tiptoes through the sleeping mutts in the middle of the night. They're rudely awakened by an alarm clock. Tweety inquires innocently, "Now who do you suppose would want to disturb those doggies so early in the morning?"

HOPPY GO LUCKY

Sylvester, Hippety Hopper; Aug 9; LT; Directed by Robert McKimson; Story by Tedd Pierce; Animation by Charles McKimson, Herman Cohen, Rod Scribner, and Phil DeLara; Layouts by Robert Givens; Backgrounds by Richard H. Thomas; Voice Characterization by Mel Blanc; Musical Direction by Carl W. Stalling

In Sylvester's latest baby-kangaroo-sure-looks-like-a-giant-mouse fiasco, a dopey lug named Benny is his companion. Sylvester (repeatedly called George so you don't miss the *Of Mice and Men* influence) is interested in getting a meal, while Benny seeks companionship ("To have one for my very own, to love him and pet him, to hug him and hug him, pet him and pet him"). When Sylvester encounters a "giant mouse" in a dockside warehouse, Benny doesn't believe

him any more than Junior did. Each time Benny goes in the warehouse, Hoppy boots him out. Sylvester finally goes in for a look of his own and lights a candle, not realizing it's really a stick of TNT. At the end of the cartoon, Hoppy drags Benny away, and the TNT explodes in Sylvester's face.

BIRD IN A GUILTY CAGE

Tweety, Sylvester; Aug 30; LT; Directed by I. Freleng; Story by Warren Foster; Animation by Manuel Perez, Ken Champin, Virgil Ross, and Arthur Davis; Layouts by Hawley Pratt; Backgrounds by Irv Wyner; Voice Characterization by Mel Blanc; Musical Direction by Carl W. Stalling

A department store after closing time is the backdrop for Sylvester's Tweety hunt. Sylvester whistles at mannequins and introduces the bird to a game called sandwich. The cat constructs a surreal ladder of mannequin body parts to reach Tweety but the bird manages to place roller skates beneath the ladder, sending the cat downstairs; Sylvester reappears in a strange mixture of lingerie and mannequin anatomy. After several other foiled attempts, Sylvester opens his mouth to receive Tweety, but gets a stick of TNT instead. Sylvester: "Well, birds are off my diet list. That one sort of upset my stomach."

TREE FOR TWO

Oct 4; Directed by I. Freleng; Story by Warren Foster; Animation by Ken Champin, Virgil Ross, Arthur Davis, and Manuel Perez; Layouts by Hawley Pratt; Backgrounds by Irv Wyner; Voice Characterization by Mel Blanc; Musical Direction by Carl Stalling

Headline: "Black Panther Escapes Zoo." Along come two dogs, the tough Spike (in turtleneck and bowler hat, as in "A Hare Grows in Manhattan") and his hero-worshipping lackey Chester (voiced by Stan Freberg), constantly babbling about doggy activities to amuse his idol. Chester tells Spike he knows the whereabouts of a cat (Sylvester) to beat up but when the bulldog enters the alley, he encounters the panther instead of the pussycat and is repeatedly thrashed. When little Chester goes in to see for himself, Sylvester is back in place; Chester grabs Sylvester and whirls him around. Spike returns to the alley and gets clawed into slices by the panther. Chester demands that the terrified bulldog face Sylvester for his own good, and tosses the cat into an ashcan. The next shot shows the tables turned, with Spike worshipping the supercilious Chester.

SNOW BUSINESS

*Tweety, Sylvester; Jan 17; LT; Directed by I. Freleng; Story
by Warren Foster; Animation by Virgil Ross, Arthur Davis,
Manuel Perez, Ken Champin; Layouts by Hawley Pratt;
Backgrounds by Carlos Manriquez; Voice Characterization
by Mel Blanc; Musical Direction by Carl Stalling*

Granny is cut off from her cabin by a blizzard that has blocked
the roads. Her bird and cat are in the cabin and she fears they'll
starve. Correction: Tweety won't starve. The pets—good friends in this cartoon—find
closet after closet filled with birdseed. Sylvester has no intention of dying of hunger,
either and thinks of something "puddies wike to eat." He lures Tweety atop the stove
with games like sailing in a paper boat in a big tureen and skating on grease in a frying
pan. Sylvester's chase after the unsuspecting bird is interrupted by a starving mouse's
efforts to eat the pussycat, gnawing at his furry head, sticking his tail in a toaster, and
pushing him into the pot in which he is trying to cook Tweety. When Granny finally
makes it through on snowshoes, she learns she's brought only more birdseed.

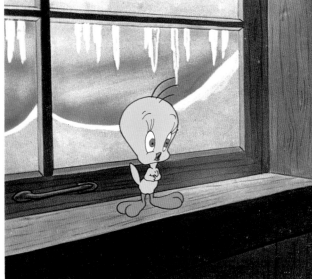

113

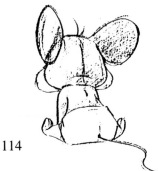

1953
A MOUSE DIVIDED

Sylvester; Jan 31; MM; Directed by I. Freleng; Story by Warren Foster; Animation by Art Davis, Manuel Perez, Ken Champin, and Virgil Ross; Layouts by Hawley Pratt; Backgrounds by Irv Wyner; Voice Characterization by Mel Blanc; Musical Direction by Carl Stalling

"A fine thing," says Sylvester. "I've become the father of a breakfast!" The ever-inebriated stork has dropped off a mouse at the home of Mr. and Mrs. Sylvester Cat. Mrs. Cat is instantly won over; Sylvester's first impulse is more carnivorous than paternal until, just as he's about to satisfy that urge (diapering the little lad in pepper and salad oil) the toddler calls him daddy. The other cats on the block don't share his fatherly affection, and when Da-Da takes baby for a stroll, the entire house is surrounded by marauding felines; Sylvester outwits them. When the stork returns to correct his mistake, his fishing rod catches Sylvester instead. The last shot shows a rather peeved Sylvester in baby get-up and carriage pushed by a mouse couple.

FOWL WEATHER

Tweety; Sylvester; Apr 4; MM; Directed by I. Freleng; Story by Warren Foster; Animation by Ken Champin, Virgil Ross, Arthur Davis, and Manuel Perez; Layouts by Hawley Pratt; Backgrounds by Irv Wyner; Voice Characterization by Mel Blanc; Musical Direction by Carl Stalling

Farm-owner Granny warns her bulldog Hector not to let anything happen to Tweety, threatening him with machine-gun fire from her umbrella. The dog foils Sylvester's first attempt to sneak up on the bird in a scarecrow disguise. Tweety says, "As long as I'm outta my cage, I might as well look around a bit" and greets the various farm animals, the moo moo cow, the dirty pig, instantly identifying a goat as the puddy in a mask. Sylvester tries to disguise himself as a chicken, but the tough head rooster calls his bluff and demands he lay an egg. When Hector hears Granny's buggy approaching the dog splashes yellow paint on Sylvester, sticks him in the cage, and yells, "Sing, you buzzard!" fooling the pixilated Granny, leading Tweety to remark, "If he's a birdie, dat makes me a puddy tat."

TOM TOM TOMCAT

Tweety, Sylvester; June 27; MM; Directed by I. Freleng; Story by Warren Foster; Animation by Ken Champin, Virgil Ross, Arthur Davis, and Manuel Perez; Layouts by Hawley Pratt; Backgrounds by Irv Wyner; Effects Animation by Harry Love; Voice Characterization by Mel Blanc; Musical Direction by Carl Stalling

As pioneers, Granny and Tweety are singing their way across the prairie when they're sighted by a tribe of Indian cats (all Sylvesters or variants) who go into a war dance before attacking the wagon, and later the fort to which the pioneers escape. Chief Rain-in-the-P-P-Puss commands a Sylvester to "scalp-um old lady squaw." The cat comes out scalped himself ("Ya got any more bright ideas?") Disguised as Sitting Bull, Granny lures the cats into the powder room and, at their request, provides them with a match so they can see where they are. In an appropriately imaginative ending, Tweety opens an umbrella as cats fall from the skies. "It's waining puddy tats."

Fowl Weather

A STREET CAT NAMED SYLVESTER

Tweety, Sylvester; Sept 5; LT; Directed by I. Freleng; Story by Warren Foster; Animation by Virgil Ross, Arthur Davis, Manuel Perez, and Ken Champin; Layouts by Hawley Pratt; Backgrounds by Irv Wyner; Voice Characterization by Mel Blanc; Music by Carl W. Stalling

A freezing Tweety enters the home of Sylvester and Granny. Sylvester keeps Tweety's existence from Granny so she won't interfere with his chase, but Hector the bulldog protects the bird from the puddy despite a broken leg that Granny is treating with putrid doggy medicine. Sylvester conceals Tweety in a vase, and after several bits with Granny and the dog returns to it, reaches in, and pulls out not the bird but a dynamite stick. When Tweety hides in Granny's knitting box, the cat goes in after him. Granny resumes her knitting, using Sylvester's fur; when the cat reknits himself he has a multicolored lower half. Dropping a refrigerator on Hector, Sylvester winds up with a broken leg himself, and Granny dutifully pumps the medicine into his mouth.

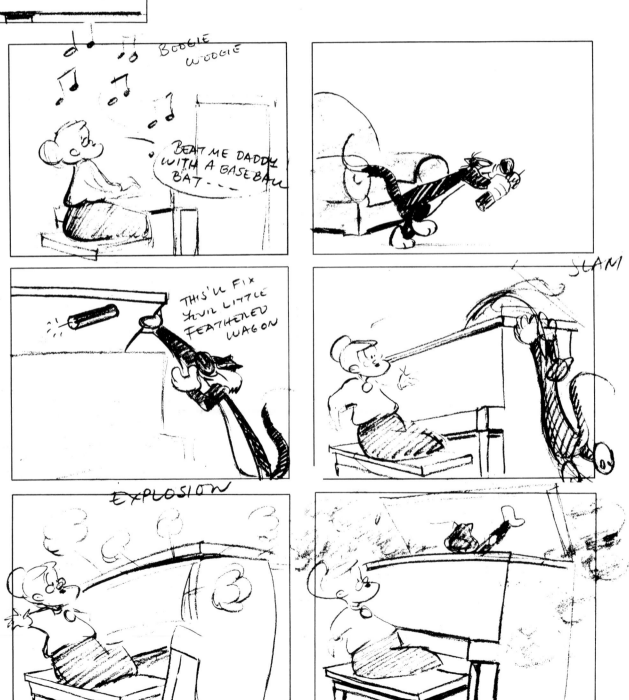

116

CATTY CORNERED

Tweety, Sylvester; Oct 31; MM; Directed by I. Freleng; Story by Warren Foster; Animation by Arthur Davis, Manuel Perez, Ken Champin, and Virgil Ross; Layouts by Hawley Pratt; Backgrounds by Irv Wyner; Voice Characterization by Mel Blanc; Musical Direction by Carl W. Stalling

"Tweety Bird Missing! Rare Bird Feared Kidnapped! Police authorities believe that Tweety Bird is being held for ransom by the notorious Rocky and his gang. And if you are listening, Rocky, don't hoit the boid!" Sylvester, about to dig into his usual trash meal hears about Tweety and starts after him, his concern more carnivorous than civic. The gangsters, Rocky and Nick (not Mugsy), deliver the trademark line, "Hey, boss, we tawt we taw a puddy tat" and send Sylvester falling into an alley. Sylvester nobly offers to let Tweety hide in his mouth and then in a can. Nick searches the pussy cat, and Rocky lets him think he's getting away with something ("Get your package and scram"). He's really switched a TNT stick for the boid. Sylvester infiltrates the gang's hideout in the dumbwaiter; the police arrive and they assume he's a hero cat. He makes the front page and is about to be decorated at city hall when he tries to take a bite out of Tweety.

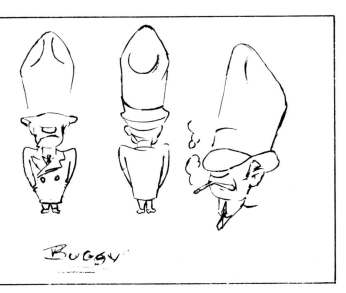

CAT'S AWEIGH

Sylvester, Junior, Hippety Hopper; Nov 28; MM; Directed by Robert McKimson;
Story by Tedd Pierce; Animation by Phil DeLara, Charles McKimson,
Herman Cohen, and Rod Scribner; Layouts by Robert Givens; Backgrounds by
Richard H. Thomas; Voice Characterization by Mel Blanc; Musical Direction
by Carl W. Stalling

Freeloaders Sylvester and Junior are ship's cats. Sylvester goofs off on the pretence that "You're a little cat so you take care of the little mice. I'm a big cat, so I take care of big ones, if any come along. Fair enough?" In the hold, a little mouse runs into a cage marked, "Baby Kangaroo," and Junior unknowingly releases Hippety Hopper, who looks like a "great giant mouse." We're off to the races yet again. Sylvester tries rushing the kangaroo with Harpo Marx-style fisticuffs, but only gets tossed out so he can indulge in some witty repartee with Junior ("Did you give him his just desserts, Father?" "No. He doesn't like desserts!"). Then Sylvester changes his tune: "Look, Son, there's a whole mess of little mice, and only one big one. So it's only fair for me to round up the little ones, and you take care of the big one." Junior enters the hold cautiously and realizes Hippety is mimicking his actions. He tricks Hippety back into his cage.

Sylvester pursues a little mouse, telling Junior, "No matter what you hear, don't open this door!" Upon running into a ferocious creature in the next room, Sylvester screams for Junior to open the door. The beast slams Sylvester into the steel walls, making Sylvester imprints and leading Junior to observe, "That's what makes me proud of my Pop. Wherever he goes, he always makes a good impression."

1954
DOG POUNDED

Tweety, Sylvester; Jan 2; LT; Directed by I. Freleng; Story by Warren Foster; Animation by Manuel Perez, Ken Champin, and Arthur Davis; Layouts by Hawley Pratt; Backgrounds by Irv Wyner; Voice Characterization by Mel Blanc; Musical Direction by Carl W. Stalling

This funny series of blackout gags has Tweety's nest in the middle of the city dog pound, with hundreds of vicious bulldog Tweetie-protectors just waiting for Sylvester to try and cross their yard so they can make mincemeat of him. Among the highlights are Sylvester walking across a tight rope holding an umbrella for balance, the dogs collectively blowing a wind of doggie-breath at him; Sylvester trying mass hypnotism to knock out the pooches, but Tweety tricking him into blurting out the secret of how to restore them to normal; Sylvester tiptoeing through the apparently empty yard and then climbing Tweety's tree only to discover the bulldogs all sitting on branches. At last, Sylvester manages to scare them off with a phoney skunk stripe painted down his back, but as he is grabbing Tweety, Pepe LePew arrives out of nowhere to make love to him.

BELL HOPPY

Sylvester, Hippety Hopper; Apr 17; MM: Directed by Robert McKimson; Story by Tedd Pierce; Animation by Charles McKimson, Herman Cohen, Rod Scribner, and Phil DeLara; Layouts by Robert Givens; Backgrounds by Richard H. Thomas; Voice Characterization by Mel Blanc; Musical Direction by Carl W. Stalling

A gang of alley cats tries to make a chump out of Sylvester with Hippety hopping into the middle of it. Sylvester dearly wants to become a member of the "Loyal Order of Alley Cats Mouse and Chowder Club," but he keeps getting blackballed. To give him a hard time, the gang offers to initiate him into the club if he can bell a big mouse; they plan to jump the mouse as soon as they hear the bell. Hippety, having hopped away from the city zoo truck, is less than eager to be belled. Sylvester decides to "resort to a little ch-ch-chicanery." With a mirror trick, he gets Hoppy to slip on the bell and announces this to the gang. In the meantime, Hoppy has been caught by the zoo keeper, and the cats unwittingly jump an oncoming truck.

DR. JERKYL'S HIDE

Sylvester, Spike and Chester; May 8; LT; Directed by I. Freleng; Story by Warren Foster; Animation by Arthur Davis, Manuel Perez, Ken Champin, and Virgil Ross; Layouts by Hawley Pratt; Backgrounds by Irv Wyner; Voice Characterization by Mel Blanc; Musical Direction by Carl W. Stalling

Spike (called Alfie) mistreats his "pal" Chester, until the two cockney canines encounter a true terror of a Sylvester. They wake the slumbering Sylvester, and he flees into the lab of one Dr. Jerkyl. There, thirsty and out of breath, the cat consumes some of the infamous Hyde formula. As the monster, the cat scratches Alf to little pieces, then turns back to Sylvester before the little dog sees him. Chester pushes Alf back in for his own good. When Alf sees Sylvester bolting out the window he thinks he can win back his reputation with phony fight noises. A fly gets a drop of the Hyde juice and turns into a behemoth that pummels Alf.

CLAWS FOR ALARM

Porky Pig, Sylvester; May 22; MM; Directed by Charles M. Jones; Story by Michael Maltese; Animation by Lloyd Vaughan, Ken Harris, Ben Washam, Abe Levitow, and Richard Thompson; Layouts by Maurice Noble; Backgrounds by Philip DeGuard; Voice Characterization by Mel Blanc; Musical Direction by Carl W. Stalling

"This looks like a perfectly splendid place to spend the night, doesn't it, Sylvester?" asks Porky. "It's so quaint and picturesque." The naive pig attributes the lack of people on the streets and in the lobby to everyone's being asleep. The frightened feline realizes this is a haunted hotel in the middle of a ghost town. As the two walk up the steps, murderous mice eyes are upon them, and strange things begin to happen. The pig attributes the commotion to Sylvester. A rope is lowered around his neck, Sylvester cuts it, and Porky wakes to find the cat holding the noose in one hand and a razor in the other. A killer mouse swings on a rope Tarzan-style; others gang up to make a sheeted ghost. Porky never gets wise. The bloodshot-eyed Sylvester must guard Porky with a rifle all night, and when the rested pig wakes up and announces they may stay for a week the petrified pussycat clobbers him, and the two drive away (with little killer eyes appearing behind the dashboard).

122

MUZZLE TOUGH

*Tweety, Sylvester; June 26; MM: Directed by I. Freleng; Story by
Warren Foster; Animation by Ken Champin, Virgil Ross, Arthur Davis,
and Manuel Perez; Layouts by Hawley Pratt; Backgrounds by Irv
Wyner; Voice Characterization by Mel Blanc; Musical Direction by
Carl W. Stalling*

Sylvester can scarcely believing his eyes when he sees movers carrying a
birdcage into a brownstone that Granny is moving into. Sylvester tries
sneaking in disguised as a lamp and then as one of the moving men. Tweety
directs him as he carries a piano up the stairs ("My, but you're stwong")
and out the attic window, leaving him with piano keyboard teeth ("That
last step was a wuwu"). Next the cat puts on a bearskin rug, which Tweety
enjoys ("Oh, wook! A cute wittle teddy-bear coming to pway wiff me!")
and Granny shoots. To get past the dog, the cat dons a female dog costume, swiveling his hips to "It Had to Be You." Before he can mallet the
dog, he's netted by the dog catcher and carried off. Sylvester takes off his
suit to show the catcher he's really a cat, attracting the immediate interest
of the real dogs in the van.

SATAN'S WAITIN'

Tweety, Sylvester; Aug 7; LT; Directed by I. Freleng; Story by Warren Foster; Animation by Virgil Ross, Arthur Davis, Manuel Perez, and Ken Champin; Layouts by Hawley Pratt; Backgrounds by Irv Wyner; Voice Characterization by Mel Blanc; Musical Direction by Carl W. Stalling

In the course of chasing Tweety, Sylvester falls off a building—and dies! His ghostly spirit goes to Hades to await his other eight lives. A satanic bulldog goads Sylvester into losing his other lives, encouraging him to chase the canary into the most violent situations. Sylvester loses life #2 getting flattened by a steamroller; the cat is scared to death in an amusement park fun house, loses four more lives in a shooting gallery, and life #8 on a roller coaster. Determined to be more careful, Sylvester stops chasing Tweety and camps out in a bank vault. That night, thieves blow the vault open, killing themselves and Sylvester!

BY WORD OF MOUSE

Sylvester; Oct 2; LT; Directed by I. Freleng; Story by Warren Foster; Animation by Gerry Chiniquy, Art Davis, Ben Washam, and Ted Bonnicksen; Layouts by Hawley Pratt; Backgrounds by Irv Wyner; Voice Characterization by Mel Blanc; Musical Direction by Milt Franklyn.

This was the first of three annual pro-American-economic-system cartoons sponsored by the philanthropic Sloane Foundation.

In the little town of Knockwurst on der Rye, Hans tells his family about his trip to America, where he was confused by the "lamps, clamps, postage stamps, roasters, coasters, electric toasters." He is taken to a lecture at Putnell University (Old P.U.). where a mouse/professor expounds the American mass-market phenomenon between rounds of being chased by Sylvester, the cat seeking to eliminate the middle stages of American retail in favor of a more direct connection with his food chain, "mouse consumption."

1955
LIGHTHOUSE MOUSE

Sylvester; Hippety Hopper; Mar 12; MM; Directed by Robert McKimson; Story by Sid Marcus; Animation by Phil DeLara, Charles McKimson, Herman Cohen, and Rod Scribner; Layouts by Robert Givens; Backgrounds by Richard H. Thomas; Voice Characterization by Mel Blanc; Music by Milt Franklyn

A little mouse's sleep is disturbed by the light from a lighthouse. He unplugs the light, causing a ship to accidentally dump some cargo—a crate containing Hippety Hopper. The lighthouse-keeper, a Scotsman, orders his cat Sylvester to catch the "crazy moose that is loose in the hoose." Up in the lamp room, Sylvester catches not the pipsqueak mouse, but the kangaroo. Misbelieving his eyes, he douses himself with vitamins. Sylvester tries to keep the light on, Hippety and the tiny mouse keep trying to turn it off; in one funny bit, opening and closing doors alternately reveal Sylvester thrashing the little mouse and the giant mouse thrashing Sylvester. The last shot shows rotating Sylvester, rigged with a battery, searchlight beams emitting from his eyes.

SANDY CLAWS

Tweety; Sylvester; Apr 2; LT; Directed by I. Freleng;
Story by Arthur Davis and Warren Foster; Animation
by Art Davis, Manel Perez, and Virgil Ross;
Layouts by Hawley Pratt; Backgrounds by Irv
Wyner; Voice Characterization by Mel Blanc;
Musical Direction by Carl W. Stalling

Granny leaves Tweety on the beach while she goes to change into her "bikini bathing suit." Sylvester sees Tweety and goes after him, but an enormous wave takes the bird first and traps him on a rock in the middle of the sea. Sylvester tries to "save" him—with fishing reel, motorboat, skis, and waterwings—but the water is full of sharks, and Sylvester is repeatedly bitten. Granny applauds "that wonderful brave cat trying to save my little bird," and suggests that he should be rewarded—but, as Tweety rows to shore, Sylvester, now with a parachute, is lowered into the dog pound.

Sandy Claws

TWEETY'S CIRCUS

Tweety, Sylvester; June 4; MM; Directed by I. Freleng; Story by Warren Foster; Animation by Arthur Davis, Gerry Chiniquy, and Ted Bonnicksen; Layouts by Hawley Pratt; Backgrounds by Irv Wyner; Voice Characterization by Mel Blanc; Music by Milt Franklyn.

To Sylvester's delight, the circus includes a Tweety Bird along with tigers, elephants and lions. But Sylvester manages to annoy the other animals—razzing a caged lion for being billed as "king of cats," hiding in an elephant's trunk—so that they deter his efforts to catch the little bird. The lion and the elephant go after Sylvester and he must exploit his abilities as high-diver, fire-eater and high-wire walker to avoid them. Just when he thinks he's free, he finds himself locked in the lion cage. Tweety calls the audience to enjoy "fifty wions and one puddy tat," but after a ferocious roar, the spiel becomes "fifty wions, count 'em, fifty wions."

JUMPIN' JUPITER

Porky Pig, Sylvester; Aug 6; MM; Directed by Charles M. Jones; Story by Michael Maltese; Animation by Ken Harris, Keith Darling; Abe Levitow, and Richard Thompson; Effects Animation by Harry Love; Layouts by Robert Givens; Backgrounds by Philip DeGuard; Voice Characterization by Mel Blanc; Musical Direction by Carl Stalling

During a vacation in a western desert, Sylvester's fear of coyotes marks him as a cowardly cat even before a buzzard from the planet Jupiter tries to capture him and Porky as an example of earthling animal life. The alien bores a hole under their tent, and takes the whole patch of earth, including Porky, Sylvester, their tent and their car, into space. Porky somehow doesn't notice the change, or even the lack of gravity; Sylvester is petrified, all reaction shots. Somehow, the tent and car drift back to land. In the morning, Porky remarks that "things sure look different after a good's night's sleep—still unaware that they are no longer on Earth.

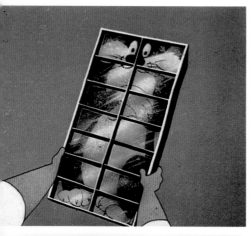

A KIDDIE'S KITTY

Sylvester; Aug 20; MM; Directed by I. Freleng; Story by Warren Foster; Animation by Arthur Davis, Gerry Chiniquy, and Ted Bonnicksen; Layouts by Hawley Pratt; Backgrounds by Irv Wyner; Music by Milt Franklyn

An abusive little girl named Suzanne want a real cat to play with. Sylvester is chased into her yard by a vicious bulldog and allows himself to be adopted to escape. Suzanne hugs (chokes) him, puts him through the washing machine and dryer, throws him in the freezer to hide him from her mother, and then thaws him with an electric blanket that fries him. After feeding him liver and sardines made of mud, she sends him, via a swing back into the hands of the dogs. Then she blasts him into space. When Suzanne's mother tells her she can keep the cat, Sylvester runs to find the dogs he was avoiding.

SPEEDY GONZALES ACADEMY AWARD WINNER

Speedy Gonzales; Sylvester; September 17; MM; Directed by I. Freleng; Story by Warren Foster; Animation by Gerry Chiniquy, Ted Bonnicksen, and Art Davis; Layouts by Hawley Pratt; Backgrounds by Irv Wyner; Voice Characterization by Mel Blanc; Musical Direction by Carl W. Stalling.

Speedy comes to the aid of hungry Mexican mice who are kept out of a cheese factory by Sylvester. Four scenes deserve mention: Sylvester caught in a series of mouse-traps he's laid for Speedy; the mouse hiding inside a baseball; Sylvester in a field of landmines, which go off as soon as he thinks he's safe; and the mouse running into Sylvester's mouth and out through his tail. In the end, Sylvester blows up the factory to keep the mice from getting in—and the cheese falls all over them.

RED RIDING HOODWINKED

Tweety, Sylvester; Oct 29; LT; Directed by I. Freleng; Story by Warren Foster; Animation by Arthur Davis, Gerry Chiniquy, and Ted Bonnicksen; Layouts by Hawley Pratt; Backgrounds by Irv Wyner; Voice Characterization by Mel Blanc; Music by Milt Franklyn

In this modernized version of the fairy tale, Red takes a bus to visit Granny, bringing a Tweety bird that has attracted Sylvester's attention. The bus lets her off far from her destination, so she must walk through the woods and meet a hungry, but absent-minded wolf, who must be reminded of his mission in life by signs. Both the Big Bad Wolf and the Big Bad Puddy Tat are in Granny's house when Red and Tweety get there. They go through the famous dialogue in duplicate. After slapstick antics, girl and bird flee on a bus, but the wolf and cat are thrown off by Granny in the guise of bus driver Ralph Kramden.

HEIR CONDITIONED

Elmer Fudd, Sylvester; Nov 26; LT; Directed by Friz Freleng; Story by Warren Foster; Animation by Art Davis, Gerry Chiniquy, and Virgil Ross; Layouts by Hawley Pratt; Backgrounds by Irv Wyner: Voice Characterization by Mel Blanc; Music by Milt Franklyn

A cat in an alley sees a newspaper and reads, "Pet Cat Inherits Fortune." Sylvester and his alley cat cronies try to sneak a satchel of loot past Elmer Fudd so they can have a high old time, re-using the hole in the floor and something-or-other cleaner company bits from "A Mouse Divided." The sponsor (Sloane Foundation) has a more serious message: Fudd pweaches how Sylvester's investment of the "idle cash" he's inherited from his late owner will lead to new pwoducts, new industwies, and a higher standard of living. Fudd takes out a projector to show on film how savings lead to capital investments that have helped everyone (anticipating the same scene in Kurt Vonnegut's *Player Piano*) and converts the alley cats. When Sylvester gets the money to them, they scold him, "What are you tryin' to do, upset our whole economic structure? PUT IT BACK!" Sylvester finally agrees to invest it, snarling at a shot of the old lady, "Sakes! You'd'a saved me a lotta trouble if you'd'a figured out a way to take it with you."

PAPPY'S PUPPY

Sylvester; Dec 17; MM; Directed by Friz Freleng; Story by Warren Foster; Animation by Gerry Chiniquy; Layouts by Hawley Pratt; Backgrounds by Irv Wyner; Voice Characterization by Mel Blanc; Musical Direction by Carl Stalling

In a dog and cat hospital, Butch J. Bulldog nervously awaits the arrival of his son. He takes his puppy home and teaches him to walk with "a mean look" and attack cats. The puppy plays with a ball, which rolls toward Sylvester. At first, the puppy runs from the feline, but, realizing it's a cat, the puppy comes back to attack. Sylvester takes care of the little pest by putting him in a tin can. Butch rescues his son and hammers the cat into the same can. Sylvester walks across the yard, passing Butch; the little puppy plays with his tail. When the cat swats the puppy away, Butch runs after Sylvester and slaps him.

Sylvester throws a stick and the puppy fetches it. He then throws the stick into the street traffic, but the puppy returns it. Butch throws the stick back into the busy street and forces Sylvester to get it. The cat narrowly misses getting hit but is run over by a scooter on the sidewalk. Sylvester nails the pesky puppy in Butch's doghouse with a dynamite stick, but Butch replaces his son with Sylvester. Sylvester rigs a rifle trigger to a bone but just as the puppy grabs the bone, Butch walks by. Sylvester grabs the rifle, puts his finger in it, and gets blasted. The stork comes to the front gate looking for Butch with an addition to his family—a basketful of bulldog puppies.

1956
TOO HOP TO HANDLE

Sylvester; Hippety Hopper; Jan 28; LT; Directed by Robert McKimson; Story by Warren Foster; Animation by Robert McKimson and Keith Darling; Layouts and Backgrounds by Richard H. Thomas; Film Editor: Treg Brown; Voice Characterization by Mel Blanc; Music by Milt Franklyn.

Once again, the baby kangaroo escapes, and Sylvester and Junior mistake him for a giant mouse. This time, Sylvester has told Junior that he can't teach him how to catch mice because there are none around, so Junior carves a windpipe to attract mice Pied-piper style. Junior notices Hippety before Sylvester, and for once must convince his father that something is amiss. The pipe attracts other animals as well, and Sylvester ends up riding a wild pig. Junior and Sylvester see the zookeeper haul Hippety off and finally realize he is a kangaroo; Sylvester breaks the pipe in two—to attract little mice—and get a pack of bulldogs instead.

131

TWEET AND SOUR

Tweety; Sylvester; Mar 24; LT; Directed by Friz Freleng; Story by Warren Foster;
Animation by Virgil Ross, Art Davis, and Gerry Chiniquy; Layouts by Hawley Pratt;
Backgrounds by Irv Wyner; Voice Characterization by Mel Blanc (June Foray);
Music by Milt Franklyn

"Let me warn you, Sylvester," Granny threatens, "if there is one little feather, just one little feather, harmed on this bird, I'm going to sell you to the violin string factory." After Granny leaves, Tweety "air-fiddles" to remind the cat of Granny's threat. This threat encompasses other cats who are hungry for Tweety, and Sylvester has to rescue Tweety from a scroungy, one-eyed orange alley-cat. What follows is grab-the-bird-and-run back and forth between the two puddy tats, each armed with an endless arsenal of mallets and anvils. When Sylvester gets the bird back to the house, Tweety compliments him, "Say, you're weally a nice puddy tat." Sylvester counters, "I just don't relish the idea of having p-p-pizzacatos played on me in some string section." He finally gets rid of the rival cat with a few balloons carrying dynamite. Granny returns just as he's putting Tweety back in his cage. "Ah, what's the use," he sobs, falling into the violin case. "She'll never believe me."

TREE CORNERED TWEETY

Tweety, Sylvester; May 19; MM; Directed by Friz Freleng; Story by Warren Foster; Animation by Arthur Davis, Gerry Chiniquy, and Virgil Ross; Layouts by Hawley Pratt; Backgrounds by Irv Wyner; Voice Characterization by Mel Blanc; Music by Milt Franklyn

"This is the city. Three million people. Three hundred thousand puddy tats. That's where I come in. I'm a little bird. I live in a cage. My name is Tweety." Mel Blanc provides a deliciously ludicrous imitation of Jack Webb. The gags include Sylvester on skis chasing Tweety on spoons; Sylvester chasing Tweety into the automat and locating him in a slot in the dessert section marked "Tweety Pie"; Sylvester trying to tiptoe across a minefield until Tweety gives him a magnet which attracts all the explosives. Each gag is accompanied by Dragnet-type narration, ending with: "May 22, 11:20 a.m.: Colorado seemed like a place where dat puddy tat couldn't find me, but I was wrong." Sylvester chases Tweety under a wooden bridge, and falls into the boat of a passing tourist.

TUGBOAT GRANNY

Tweety, Sylvester; June 23; MM; Directed by Friz Freleng; Story by Warren Foster; Animation by Virgil Ross, Art Davis, and Gerry Chiniquy; Layouts by Hawley Pratt; Backgrounds by Irv Wyner; Film Editor: Treg Brown; Voice Characterization by Mel Blanc; Musical Direction by Milt Franklyn

Though Granny, for the only time, gets her name in the title, she only appears in the first scene, a duet with her baby bird about life on the tugboat. The rest of the film concerns Sylvester's efforts to board the tug. Tweety destroys his first boat with an anchor, his plastic raft with a dart. Attempts to jump off bridges onto the boat also fail—once when Sylvester jumps into the flaming smokestack, later when his parachute does not open until he is under water. The end of the cartoon finds him smashing into a pole, causing a fish to gurgle, "I tawt I taw a puddy tat."

THE UNEXPECTED PEST

Sylvester; June 2; MM; Directed by Robert McKimson; Story by Warren Foster; Animation by Keith Darling, Ted Bonnicksen, George Grandpre, and Russ Dyson; Layouts by Robert Gribbroek; Backgrounds by Richard H. Thomas; Film Editor: Treg Brown; Voice Characterization by Mel Blanc; Musical Direction by Carl W. Stalling

Sylvester hears his people, John and Martha, planning to get rid of him now that he's rid the house of mice. He realizes, "I've got to get a mouse to keep my happy home." He finds one and instructs it to scare the lady, who decides to keep the cat in case there are other mice around. After a successful scare, the heretofore frightened mouse tells Sylvester that "It looks like you need me—from now on it makes me the boss around here." The mouse tries dangerous stunts, knowing that Sylvester must protect him, finally sitting on a stick of TNT. After that, the bandaged cat watches the mouse fake a suicide, saying, "After all he's been through I thought he deserved a happy ending."

YANKEE DOOD IT

Sylvester; Elmer Fudd; Oct 13; MM; Directed by Friz Freleng; Story by Warren Foster; Animation by Gerry Chiniquy, Virgil Ross, and Art Davis; Layouts by Hawley Pratt; Backgrounds by Irv Wyner; Film Editor: Treg Brown; Musical Direction by Milt Franklyn

The King of Elves (Elver Fudd) sends a messenger to recall the elves who have been helping the shoemaker. The shoemaker complains that he won't be able to get his work done without the little people. Meanwhile, the hungry Sylvester runs after the messenger, who comes closer and closer to being turned into a mouse each time the shoemaker says "Jehosaphat." The King arrives and explains the fundamentals of capitalist theory. Months pass and the King returns to find the shoemaker has 500 workers and a new product—the Jehosaphat boot.

THE SLAP-HOPPY MOUSE

Sylvester, Hippety Hopper; Sept 1; MM; Directed by Robert McKimson; Story by Tedd Pierce; Animation by Ted Bonnicksen, George Grandpre, Keith Darling, and Russ Dyson; Layouts by Robert Gribbroek; Backgrounds by Richard H. Thomas; Film Editor: Treg Brown; Voice Characterization by Mel Blanc; Musical Direction by Carl W. Stalling

As pets in a mansion, Sylvester and Junior have it soft. But Junior can't stand the shame of having a has-been for a father, and to prove it isn't so, Sylvester takes Junior mouse-catching, approaching the hunt as if it were a mouse safari. Hippety Hopper, having fallen off the circus train, shows up. Junior insists that his father catch the giant mouse because, "he's only a mouse, Father, and cats aren't afraid of mice." Each attempt to lunge at Hippety gets Sylvester thrown out. Finally, Sylvester gets glued to the floor, and Junior saws out the floor around him, and carries him out.

1957

TWEET ZOO

Tweety, Sylvester; Jan 12; MM; Directed by Friz Freleng; Story by Warren Foster; Animation by Art Davis, Virgil Ross, and Gerry Chiniquy; Layouts by Hawley Pratt; Backgrounds by Irv Wyner; Film Editor: Treg Brown; Voice Characterization by Mel Blanc; Musical Direction by Milt Franklyn

Touring the zoo, the puddy tat is only interested in the Tweety Bird. Tweety's ploy is to enter the cages of more dangerous animals, under the accurate impression that Sylvester will do something to annoy them and get thrashed. When an elephant stands over a hole in which Tweety has hidden, Sylvester tries to scare an elephant with a mouse. The elephant, in fear, stomps on Sylvester. He also trespasses on the turf of the crocodile, lion, and bear, and is trounced by each. Leaving the zoo, he decides to remove birds from his diet.

TWEETY AND THE BEANSTALK

*Tweety, Sylvester; May 16; MM; Directed by Friz Freleng;
Story by Warren Foster; Animation by Virgil Ross, Gerry
Chiniquy, and Art Davis; Layouts by Hawley Pratt; Film
Editing by Treg Brown; Voice Characterization by Mel Blanc
(uncredited: June Foray); Musical Direction by Milt Franklyn*

As 1955's "Beanstalk Bunny" meshed Jones's Bugs-Daffy-Elmer with "Jack & Beanstalk" elements, Freleng's foray up the beanstalk gives an added kick to the usual Sylvester
and Tweety shenanigans by having Sylvester go through his old tricks in a giant world
against a giant Tweety ("acres and acres of Tweety bird!") and a giant bulldog. Sylvester
tries reaching Tweety with a casting rod (tying one end to his tail and reeling himself
up, ending in a giant mousehole meeting a giant mouse). He unscrews the bottom of
the bird's giant cage with a screwdriver on a stick, then pops up on a flying champagne
cork. After getting caught between the giant bulldog's deathly percussive games, he
manages to grab the bird, thanks to a makeshift catapult that backfires. Anyway, the
giant returns ("Fee fo fi fat—I tawt I taw a puddy tat") and chases Sylvester down the
beanstalk. The cat chops it so the giant plummets, landing right on Sylvester and pushing him straight through the ground to China, where he is observed by a coolie-Tweety,
who tawt he "taw honolable puddy tat."

BIRDS ANONYMOUS

Tweety, Sylvester; Aug 10; MM; Directed by Friz Freleng; Story by Warren Foster; Animation by Art Davis, Virgil Ross, and Gerry Chiniquy; Layouts by Hawley Pratt; Backgrounds by Boris Gorelick; Film Editing by Treg Brown; Voice Characterization by Mel Blanc; Musical Direction by Milt Franklyn

"Birds Anonymous" is the pussycat's equivalent of Alcoholics Anonymous, with cats testifying to addictions and supporting one another in their efforts to "kick the bird habit." This is carried out beautifully, with Freleng getting under the skin of Sylvester, who for once devotes all his energy and brainpower to *not* eating Tweety, going "cold turkey" or, rather, "cold Tweety." Nothing helps. To get birds off his mind, he turns on the TV and finds a cooking program describing the delights of roast birds, and the radio plays songs like "Bye Bye Blackbird" and "When the Red Red Robin . . ." He tries chaining himself to the radiator so he "won't be able to get the bird," but Tweety's

confused query, "Oh, Mr. Puddy-Tat, don't you wike me anymore?" drives him wild enough to heave the entire radiator from the wall! Fortunately, his comrade from B. A. fires a plunger into his face. That night, Sylvester tosses and turns, his eyes red with bird desire, "Just one little bird, no one'll know the difference . . . Then I'll quit." Again the B. A. cat (later identified as "Sam") helps him stop. By this point, he's a craven, blubbering addict. "I gotta have a bird! I'm weak but I don't care! I can't help it! After all, I am a pussy cat." The B. A. cat's demonstration of how birds and cats can live together in peace involves his kissing Tweety and thus getting a taste of bird and soon wanting more . . . "Once a bad ol' puddy tat, always a bad old puddy tat."

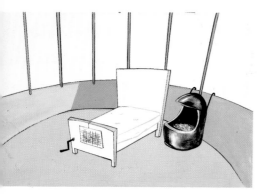

GREEDY FOR TWEETY

Tweety, Sylvester; Sept 28; LT; Directed by Friz Freleng; Story by Warren Foster; Animation by Gerry Chiniquy, Art Davis, and Virgil Ross; Layouts by Hawley Pratt; Backgrounds by Boris Gorelick; Film Editing by Treg Brown; Voice Characterization by Mel Blanc; Musical Direction by Milt Franklyn

Despite being in the hospital, and despite their cumbersome casts, Tweety, Sylvester, and the bulldog refuse to give up their respective chasings, and have no qualms about slamming one another's broken limbs with the biggest objects available. After Granny removes Tweety from the cat's stomach, and a mouse hammers both their legs, Granny decides to strap cat and dog into their beds so they can't hurt each other. Sylvester's bed-ridden "hobby" becomes constructing a mechanical device that drills a hole in the dog's cast and inserts a stick of dynamite. The dog, however, switches casts with Sylvester just before the stuff goes off. Granny picks this moment to announce that they're being released from the hospital. When she looks out the window and sees that the dog, cat, and canary are running back into traffic, all she has to say is "Que sera."

MOUSE-TAKEN IDENTITY

Sylvester, Junior, Hippety Hopper; Nov 16; MM; Directed by Robert McKimson; Story by Tedd Pierce; Animation by George Grandpre and Ted Bonnicksen; Layouts by Robert Gribbroek; Backgrounds by Bill Butler; Film Editing by Treg Brown; Voice Characterization by Mel Blanc; Musical Direction by Carl W. Stalling and Milt Franklyn

Sylvester is lucky enough to bring Junior along on a mouse hunt at the County Museum on the day that Hippety Hopper has escaped from a nearby zoo and has taken refuge in a stuffed kangaroo's pouch. When Junior is ashamed to learn that the mice who've been giving his Pop such a hard time over the years are such tiny things, Sylvester snow jobs: "You see, son, mice come in assorted sizes. Little runties, like the ones around here, and king-sized mice like I used to hunt." On hearing this, Junior points out that the big stuffed kangaroo must be an example of the latter when Hippety emerges from the pouch. The ensuing chase around the museum has Sylvester repeatedly tossed out of a cave in a prehistoric exhibit, getting bludgeoned and shot by his well-meaning son who tries to "save" him from a mounted lion head, and being scalped in an American Indian exhibit. In the windup, Sylvester crossbows himself into an Egyptian display. Junior gushes, "Oh, father, now you can be my daddy and my mummy too!"

GONZALES' TAMALES

Sylvester; Nov 30; MM; Directed by Friz Freleng; Story by Warren Foster; Animation by Art Davis, Virgil Ross, and Gerry Chiniquy; Layouts by Hawley Pratt; Backgrounds by Boris Gorelick; Film Editing by Treg Brown; Voice Characterization by Mel Blanc; Musical Direction by Carl Stalling and Milt Franklyn

When Pedro and Manuel get jealous of Speedy's success with the girls, the male mice "get an idea": to clout Sylvester with a rock and forged note-threat from Speedy. Sylvester pays a call on Speedy, who immediately carries out the note's threat. Sylvester's failed attempts at revenge include Speedy disassembling Sylvester's rifle one piece at a time, a live-grenade toss, and a wind-up senorita doll that lures Speedy out. In a last attempt, Sylvester tries to eat his way through a pile of hot peppers that Speedy is hiding in, and when his water is switched with Tabasco sauce, we close as we opened, with Pedro and Manuel discussing the airborne Sylvester. "...ees eet a bird? A plane? No, eet ees the gringo pussycat."

1958
A PIZZA TWEETY PIE

Tweety, Sylvester; Feb 22; LT; Directed by Friz Freleng; Story by Warren Foster; Animation by Virgil Ross, Gerry Chiniquy, and Art Davis; Layouts by Hawley Pratt; Backgrounds by Tom O'Loughlin; Film Editor: Treg Brown; Voice Characterization by Mel Blanc; Musical Direction by Milt Franklyn.

While in Italy with Granny, Tweety gets hounded by an Italian Sylvester, who is trying to get across the canal to get to the canary. After his gondola sinks, he tries a rubber raft, but Tweety bursts it, shrinking it tightly around the cat's rear-end. Other failed attempts follow, the final one being Sylvester's trying to water-ski after them and reel Tweety in with a fishing pole, but he bangs into a bridge when he fails to read its sign— "ducka your head—Lowla Bridgeada." When the cat tries one more time, using a strand of spaghetti as a lasso, he is bopped over the head by a mallet Granny has hidden in the pasta.

 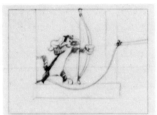  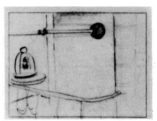

  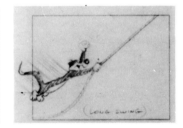 

  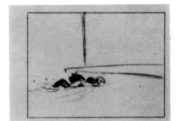 

A BIRD IN A BONNET

Tweety, Sylvester; Sept 27; MM; Directed by Friz Freleng; Story by Warren Foster; Animation by Gerry Chiniquy, Art Davis, and Virgil Ross; Layouts by Hawley Pratt; Backgrounds by Tom O'Loughlin; Film Editor: Treg Brown; Voice Characterization by Mel Blanc; Musical Direction by John Seely

When Granny buys a hat that Sylvester has chased Tweety onto, Sylvester follows Granny all over New York. He approaches her in the top hat of a gentleman who makes a fresh remark, and Granny clouts both of them with her umbrella. In Lacy's Department Store he makes it into the elevator just in time to have his tail stretched a few stories, and in J.D. Denny's he absconds with the hat to a window ledge and leaps off with a balloon. Of course, Tweety bursts the balloon and Sylvester plummets into an open manhole. His most elaborate hat-grabbing effort involves a fishing rod wielded from a taxi. When he finally does get the bird, he smacks into the Holland Tunnel. Tweety: "You know, I wose more puddy tats dat way."

1959
TRICK OR TWEET

Tweety, Sylvester; Mar 21; MM; Directed by Friz Freleng; Story by Warren Foster; Animation by Art Davis, Virgil Ross, and Gerry Chiniquy; Layouts by Hawley Pratt; Backgrounds by Tom O'Loughlin; Film Editing by Treg Brown; Voice Characterization by Mel Blanc; Musical Direction by Milt Franklyn

Although Sylvester and his pal Sam have agreed to stop chasing Tweety, they both keep after the bird, trying to keep this fact from the other (they each get the bright idea of climbing the pole in a garbage can). Eventually, they return to an out-and-out rout, as Tweety says, "I may be wrong, but I just don't twust puddy-tat's honor." How true. Seconds after Tweety installs barbed wire on the pole, we hear Sylvester yelling and picking clumps of black fur off the wire, Sam trying to trampoline up on a stretched corset. Then there's Sylvester high-wire walking. When he tries a flying "Batman costume," he crashes into Sam wearing the same. Sylvester stows away on Sam's balloon, pops it so Sam can't use it again, and, as they crash, Tweety observes, "I never wealized just bein' a little bird could be so complicated."

"LET GO — HE'S MINE   HE'S MINE!"

"MINE!"

"MINE!"

"WAIT A MINUTE, SAM — HOLD IT — HOLD IT —"

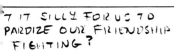

— REPEAT OF SOCKING —

"7 IT SILLY FOR US TO PARDIZE OUR FRIENDSHIP FIGHTING?"

"YEAH — I GUESS SO . . . ."

"LOOK AT WHAT WE WERE FIGHTIN'A OVER — A MISERABLE SCRAWNY LITTLE YELLA BIRD!"

"YEAH — NOT MUCH MEAT ON THAT RUNT —"

"I'VE BIN SICK —"

"— SINCE HE'S TOO LE TO DIVIDE — LOGICAL THING TO IS TO PUT HIM BACK HIS NEST + FORGET HIM!"

"REMEMBER — ON OUR HONOR AS PUSSY CATS — WE TON'T TOUCH THA BIRD!"

"PUSSY CAT'S HONOR!"

SPITS ON HAND — HITS FIST INTO HAND

"MY DOODNESS — THEY'RE NICE PUSSY CATS!"

TWEET AND LOVELY

Tweety, Sylvester; July 18; MM; Directed by Friz Freleng; Story by Warren Foster; Animation by Art Davis, Gerry Chiniquy, and Virgil Ross; Layouts by Hawley Pratt; Backgrounds by Tom O'Laughlin; Film Editing by Treg Brown; Voice Characterization by Mel Blanc; Musical Direction by Milt Franklyn.

When Sylvester realizes the only thing between him and Tweety is Spike, the bulldog, he tries a few failed projects (including a robot dog, a smoke bomb, an artificial storm cloud, and invisible paint that allows him to carry off the befuddled Tweety—"I must be walking in my sleep, but I'm not walking and I'm not sleeping. They must've repealed the law of gravity"). Spike saves the little bird by spraying yellow paint all over Sylvester. Finally, after Sylvester's last attempt explodes, he returns as an angel, declaring, "It's a good thing pussycats have got nine lives!"

CAT'S PAW

Sylvester, Sylvester, Jr.; Aug. 15; LT; Directed by Robert McKimson; Story by Tedd Pierce; Animation by George Granpre, Ted Bonnicksen, Warren Batchelder, and Tom Ray; Layouts by Robert Gribbroek; Backgrounds by William Butler; Film Editor: Treg Brown; Voice Characterizatons by Mel Blanc; Music by Milt Franklyn.

When Sylvester takes Junior bird-stalking (and after his snow-job that little ones are tougher to catch than big ones), they come across what looks like a helpless little chick but is, unbeknownst to them, a very dangerous dwarf eagle. He beats Sylvester up and terrifies him with his piercing shriek, much to the shame of his embarrassed boy. "How can I ever face the fellows in troop 12?" In the end, Sylvester tells Junior he'll have to chase butterflies or nothing, and instantly gets thrashed by a killer butterfly.

HERE TODAY, GONE TAMALE

Speedy Gonzales, Sylvester; Aug. 29; LT; Directed by Friz Freleng; Story by Michael Maltese; Animation by Gerry Chiniquy, Art Davis, and Virgil Ross; Layouts by Hawley Pratt; Backgrounds by Tom O'Loughlin; Film Editor: Treg Brown; Voice Characterization by Mel Blanc; Music by Milt Franklyn.

During a cheese famine, in which Sylvester is guarding a boat-full of the stuff from the mexican mice, Speedy Gonzales immediately comes to their rescue, and piece by piece gets the cheese down the gangplank past Sylvester. Best bits: Sylvester getting locked in the limburger storage room and turning bright blue; intending to mallet Speedy but flattening his own hand instead; getting shaved by his own guillotine. He ultimately decides to join 'em since he can't beat 'em, and, donning a pair of Mickey Mouse Club ears, leaps in the middle of the mice's flamenco dance.

TWEET DREAMS

Tweety, Sylvester; Dec. 5; MM; Directed by Friz Freleng; Story by Friz Freleng, Warren Foster; Animation by Gerry Chiniguy, Art Davis and Virgil Ross; Layouts by Hawley Bratt; Backgrounds by Tom O'Loughlin; Film Editor: Treg Brown; Voice Characterizations by Mel Blanc; Music by Milt Franklyn.

The year's second "Chapter Eleven Economy" cartoon has Sylvester seeing a psychiatrist to get the whole Tweety story off his chest. Since his father never taught him how to catch mice like all the other cats he "was forced to find sustenance by other means." That turned out to be fishing, before he ran away to the circus to forget Tweety. But Tweety turns up there and he made up his mind to get rid of the bird once and for all. "Frustration began to set in . . . " By now the doctor is asleep, and, waking, he realizes the time and that he's got to fly to Detroit ("Call me for an appointment"). He flies by flapping his arms out the window, and Sylvester follows, "Wait! Wait!"

1960
WEST OF THE PESOS

Speedy Gonzales, Sylvester; Jan. 23; MM; Directed by Robert McKimson; Story by Tedd Pierce; Animation by Tom Ray, George Grandpre, Ted Bonnicksen, and Warren Batchelder; Layouts by Robert Givens; Backgrounds by William Butler; Film Editor: Treg Brown; Voice Characterization by Mel Blanc; Music by Milt Franklin

Speedy rescues some kidnaped guinea-pig-mice, and each time Sylvester tries to foil the attempt. The cat employs a snare which Speedy pulls, dragging Sylvester through a knot-hole, getting skinned. Sylvester holds a boulder, but Speedy "Yee- Has's" causing the cat to toss the rock in the air. It lands on his head. Sylvester gets wise and sets up his mouth as a tunnel for the train to travel into. It does, right through his body and out his tail! Speedy returns the "meesing" mice and receives his reward, a kiss from a senorita, which drives him wild!

GOLDIMOUSE AND THE THREE CATS

Sylvester; Mar. 15 LT; Directed by Friz Freleng; Story by Michael Maltese; Animation by Virgil Ross, Art Davis, and Gerry Chiniquy; Layouts by Hawley Pratt; Backgrounds by Tom O'Loughlin; Film Editor: Treg Brown; Voice Characterization by Mel Blanc; Music by Milt Franklyn

When Goldimouse is found in their house, Junior goads Sylvester into catching it. Sylvester tries an arrow, which pulls the cat into the mouse hole, Mother and Junior rescuing him with a bathroom plunger, then a dart in a blowpipe, Goldimouse blowing it down Sylvester's throat and out his tail, also dynamite in a cheese trap, Sylvester falling into it, and a "better mouse trap" which catches a certain pussycat. After his last scheme causes a huge explosion, a battered Sylvester comes over to his family and dumps a bowl of porridge on his spoiled brat's head!

HYDE AND GO TWEET

Tweety, Sylvester; May 14; MM; Directed Friz Freleng; Animation by Art Davis, Gerry Chiniquy, and Virgil Ross; Layouts by Hawley Pratt; Backgrounds by Tom O'Loughlin; Film Editor: Treg Brown; Voice Characterization by Mel Blanc; Music by Milt Franklyn

When Tweety mistakenly drinks Dr. Jeckyll's formula, he becomes a giant Tweety monster terrorizing Sylvester. When Tweety returns to normal, the cat resumes the chase, always being caught with Tweety in a tight situation when the little bird reverts to "Mr. Hyde" size. At one point, when Sylvester returns to put Tweety in a sandwich, the Monster emerges from the two slices of bread and eats the cat! Sylvester jumps out of his big mouth and wakes up on the window ledge. When Tweety lands next to him, Sylvester runs through the brick wall, screaming for help!

MOUSE AND GARDEN ACADEMY AWARD NOMINEE

Sylvester; July 15; LT; Directed by Friz Freleng; Animation by Gerry Chiniquy, Virgil Ross, and Art Davis; Layouts by Hawley Pratt; Backgrounds by Tom O'Loughlin; Film Editor: Treg Brown; Voice Characterization by Mel Blanc; Music by Milt Franklyn

When Sylvester and Sam find a mouse, each one tries to get at it without the other knowing. Sylvester can't trust Sam, so he ties him to his bed. Sylvester tries for the mouse, but Sam mallets him. Sam sneaks out, and goes underwater to reach for the mouse, using a pipe for breathing. Sylvester puts a dynamite stick in the pipe! Sylvester ties Sam's tail to a motor boat, but the orange cat pulls Sylvester (and the jug) with him, water-skiing, out into the ocean. The two cats end up on a rock in the middle of the sea, kicking each other as the mouse paddles back to shore in the jug.

West of the Pesos

Goldimouse and the Three Cats

Hyde and Go Tweet

Mouse and Garden

TRIP FOR TAT

Tweety, Sylvester; Oct. 29; MM; Directed by Friz Freleng; Story by Michael Maltese; Animation by Gerry Chiniquy, Virgil Ross, and Tom Ray; Layouts by Hawley Pratt; Backgrounds by Tom O'Loughlin; Film Editor: Treg Brown; Voice Characterization by Mel Blanc; Music by Milt Franklyn

Sylvester tags along on Granny and Tweety's world trip, and a worldwide chase ensues: in Paris, Granny is "fingerpainting." Tweety also tries art, drawing a picture of the bad 'ol puddy tat. When Sylvester sticks his face where Tweety's drawing has been, the bird erases the ugly face. In the Swiss Alps, Granny and Tweety go skiing. Sylvester follows and gets clobbered by a tree. In Japan, Sylvester gets caught by a fisherman. In Italy, he somehow flies into a jackhammer and gets squashed. The cat dines at an Italian restaurant, crosses fowl off his diet menu, and digs into a big plate of spaghetti.

1961
CANNERY WOE

Speedy Gonzales, Sylvester; Jan. 7; LT; Directed by Robert McKimson; Story by Tedd Pierce; Animation by George Granpre, Ted Bonnicksen, Warren Batchelder, and Tom Ray; Layouts by Robert Gribbroek; Backgrounds by William Butler; Film Editor: Treg Brown; Effects Animation by Harry Love. Voice Characterization by Mel Blanc; Music by Milt Franklyn

When the mice can't get cheese for their rally because of Sylvester, José and Manuel have a plan: they will recruit Speedy Gonzales in exchange for political favors. Speedy races to the cheese shop. Sylvester, underestimating the little rodent, plays along and lets him in the store. Speedy runs under the cat, tearing off his fur, leaving a message, "Speedy was here!" Sylvester runs out of the shop and Speedy rips his rear with the message, "Also Here!" Speedy presents four wedges of cheese to the Mayor and races back for more. Sylvester spreads tacks, uses a cannon, and sets a whole room full of mouse traps, to no avail.

HOPPY DAZE

Sylvester, Hippety Hopper; Feb. 11; LT; Directed by Robert McKimson; Story by Tedd Pierce; Animation by Ted Bonnicksen, Warren Batchelder, Tom Ray, and George Grandpre; Layouts by Robert Gribbroek; Backgrounds by Bob Singer; Effects Animation by Harry Love; Film Editor: Treg Brown; Voice Characterization by Mel Blanc; Music by Milt Franklyn

On the advice of his "coach," Sylvester chases a mouse into a crate which happens to contain Hippety Hopper, whom Sylvester mistakes for a giant mouse. The kangaroo decks Sylvester on the dock. Each time his coach sends him in, the "giant mouse" bounces him back. ("If it keeps up like this, the kid'll make a vege-tanarian's outa me!"). The tough mouse tells Sylvester to keep his "left" up. Sylvester springs after Hoppy on a bed spring hopping into a smoke stack (all the while keeping his left up). Hoppy passes the dazed cat on the dock.

BIRDS OF A FATHER

Sylvester; Apr. 1; LT; Directed by Robert Mckimson; Story by Dave Detiege; Animation by Warren Batchelder, George Grandpre, and Ted Bonnicksen; Layouts by Robert Gribbroek; Backgrounds by William Butler; Film Editor: Treg Brown; Voice Characterization by Mel Blanc; Music by Milt Franklyn

When Sylvester finds out his son is friendly with birds, he decides to show him how to catch a bird "like a true sportsman." They go hunting with a rifle; each attempt ends in disaster. Sylvester shoots a badminton bird, and gets hit with the racquet. Sylvester shoots a bird off the hat of a lady who clobbers him with her umbrella ("She's about as helpless as a porcupine a nudist colony!"). The lisping pussycat uses a radio-controlled jetplane, but the bird returns a full-sized bullet-spraying jet fighter back at the feline. Junior introduces a new friend to his dad, Spike (his little bird friend) in kitten disguise!

D'FIGHTIN' ONES

Sylvester; Apr. 22; MM; Directed by Friz Freleng; Animation by Gerry Chiniquy, Virgil Ross, and Art Davis; Layouts by Hawley Pratt; Backgrounds by Tom O'Loughlin; Film Editor: Treg Brown; Voice Characterization by Mel Blanc; Music by Milt Franklyn.

In a spoof of a current hit film, "The Defiant Ones," Sylvester and a tough bulldog are handcuffed together, and escape from a truck taking them to the city pound. First the dog drags Sylvester through the swamps and woods, and then Sylvester gets even by chasing a mouse and dragging the pooch. They try to remove thecuffs, but each try leads to disaster. Finally, they remove their chains by hanging on a precipice, letting a train cut their bonds. They fall into the city dump and cheer, but their freedom is short-lived. Both have their legs caught in a pipe!

REBEL WITHOUT CLAWS

Tweety, Sylvester; July 15; LT; Written and Directed by Friz Freleng; Animation by Virgil Ross, Art Davis, and Gerry Chiniquy; Layouts by Hawley Pratt; Backgrounds by Tom O'Loughlin; Film Editor: Treg Brown; Voice Characterization by Mel Blanc; Music by Milt Franklyn

In the Confederate Army all the carrier pigeons have been shot down, leaving only Tweety to get a message through to headquarters. The Yankees send out their secret messenger destroyer, Sylvester, after the bird. The little bird says, "Tawt I taw a damn Yankee Tat!" and runs through the Civil War battlefield pursued by Sylvester who ends up full of holes!

Sylvester is blasted by a record number of cannons as he chases the yellow canary, including a re-do of the cannon gags in "Buccaneer Bunny." Tweety gets through the enemy lines, but encounters Sylvester dressed as a Confederate general. Tweety is sent to a firing squad ("I regret I have only one life to give to my country"), but inept Yankees shoot Sylvester! The cat remarks, "It's a good thing I have nine lives. With this kind of army, I'll need all of 'em!"

THE PIED PIPER OF GUADALUPE

ACADEMY AWARD NOMINEE

Speedy Gonzales, Sylvester; Aug. 19; LT; Directed by Friz Freleng; Co-Directed by Hawley Pratt; Story by John Dunn; Animation by Gerry Chiniquy, Virgil Ross, and Bob Matz; Backgrounds by Tom O'Loughlin; Film Editor: Treg Brown; Voice Characterization by Mel Blanc. Music by Milt Franklyn

Sylvester, chasing mice in a Mexican town, gets no respect. The mice laugh in his face, hit him with boards carrying picket signs like "Loco El Gato!" and outrun him. Seeing a book on the "Pied Piper" Sylvester dresses up like one and hypnotizes the mice into dancing into his jug.

Speedy Gonzales resists and begins to rescue his friends, one by one. Sylvester tries to stop the racing rodent with dynamite, but Speedy turns a bulldog on the cat. Sylvester chases Speedy on a motorcycle, but the mouse leads the "gato" off a cliff. The cat comes out of the infirmary on stilts and bandaged, while Speedy heckles Sylvester by playing his flute.

THE LAST HUNGRY CAT

Tweety, Sylvester; Dec. 2; MM; Directed by Friz Freleng. Co-Directed by Hawley Pratt; Story by John Dunn and Dave Detiege; Animation by Gerry Chiniquy, Virgil Ross, Bob Matz, Art Leonardi, and Lee Halpern. Backgrounds by Tom O' Loughlin; Film Editor: Treg Brown; Voice Characterization by Mel Blanc; Music by Milt Franklyn.

In a spoof of "Alfred Hitchcock Presents," a large figure of a bear in silhouette presents "tonight's story about a murder." While Tweety is sleeping in his birdcage, Sylvester sneaks up to grab the bird but trips and falls, and, fearing Granny, runs through the alley. The narrator speaks to the cat, "Sardines and milk weren't enough, you had to commit murder!" Sylvester sees a newspaper headline (Police hunt "the Cat") and runs in panic, heckled by the Hitchcock narrator accusing him of murdering Tweety. Sylvester turns on the radio and hears "Your local company will now present gas chamber music, I mean, your local gas company will present chamber music.") His guilty conscience makes Sylvester wear a groove in the floor pacing, gulping down pots of coffee, smoking a pack of cigarettes. He can't sleep and downs a dozen sleeping pills, sobbing "Other cats have eaten birds"! That narrator suggests that Sylvester give himself up. Sylvester runs back to Granny and finds Tweety alive. He kisses the little canary, Granny hitting him with her broom. Sylvester gets even with "Hitchcock" by beaning him with a brick!

1962
FISH AND SLIPS

Sylvester; Mar. 10; LT; Directed by Robert McKimson; Story by Dave Detiege; Animation by Warren Batchelder, George Granpre, and Ted Bonnicksen; Layouts and Backgrounds by Robert Gribbroek; Film Editor: Treg Brown; Voice Characterization by Mel Blanc; Music by Milt Franklyn.

After seeing a television broadcast about a fisherman (Mr. Treg Brown), Sylvester boasts to his son about being a top cat fisherman. He takes Junior to the aquarium, and uses his tail as a fishing line. He puts his tail in the pirana tank, and gets it chewed. He goes into a tank with a hammerhead and shovelnose and gets pounded into a hole! Junior catches a small fish which Sylvester uses as bait for a larger fish. He dangles it over a huge tank and gets swallowed by a whale! The lisping pussycat make a fire, and the whale spits him out. A pair of dolphin catch the cat and play catch with him. Sylvester gives it another try in a diving suit. Electric eels, lobsters, and an octopus attack him. Junior is distracted from pumping air to his father, almost choking him. Junior pumps faster to compensate, and blows up his father's diving suit. This lands the cat in the "dogfish" tank. "No matter what father tries to do, he always winds up going to the dogs!"

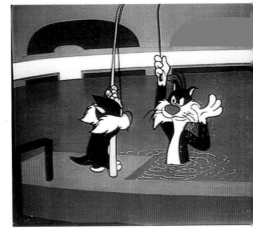

MEXICAN BOARDERS

Speedy Gonzeles, Sylvester; May 12; LT; Directed by Friz Freleng; Co-Directed by Hawley Pratt; Story by John Dunn; Animation by Gerry Chiniquy, Virgil Ross, Bob Matz, Art Leonardi, and Lee Halpern; Backgrounds by Tom O'Loughlin; Film Editor: Treg Brown; Voice Characterization by Mel Blanc; Music by Milt Franklyn.

When Speedy's cousin Slowpoke arrives, Speedy tries to get him some food. Speedy races out and back with some cheese. Now Slowpoke wants Tabasco Sauce. Speedy races for it, and when Sylvester tries to eat the mouse, Speedy pours the Tabasco Sauce in his mouth. Sylvester tries to catch Speedy with a wire net screen, but the mouse runs right through it. When Sylvester tries, he gets cut into cubes! That night, Slowpoke goes to the refrigerator for a midnight snack. Sylvester grabs him, but Slowpoke hypnotizes Sylvester into being a fan-waving slave for their late night meal.

THE JET CAGE

Tweety, Sylvester; Sept 22; LT; Written and Directed by Friz Freleng; Animation by Gerry Chiniquy, Art Leonardi, Virgil Ross, Lee Halpern, and Bob Matz; Layouts by Hawley Pratt; Backgrounds by Tom O'Loughlin; Film Editor: Treg Brown; Voice Characterization by Mel Blanc, June Foray; Music by Milt Franklyn

After Granny buys Tweety a jet powered cage, Sylvester tries to capture the bird with a butterfly net, but gets dragged along the yard, crashing into a pole. Tweety lands to get more instructions and returns to his cage. Sylvester hides inside. Tweety takes off again, and ejects the cat through the bombbay. Sylvester doesn't give up and he employs a fishing rod with magnet which "hooks" the jet cage but drags the cat into street traffic where he gets hit by a truck. He tries two fans which permit the cat to fly, but when he drops the fans to grab Tweety, he falls.

1963

MEXICAN CAT DANCE

Speedy Gonzales, Sylvester; Apr. 20; LT; Directed by Friz Freleng; Story by John Dunn; Animation by Gerry Chiniquy, Virgil Ross, Bob Matz, Lee Halpern, and Art Leonardi; Layouts by Hawley Pratt; Backgrounds by Tom O'Loughlin; Film Editor: Treg Brown; Voice Characterization by Mel Blanc; Music by Bill Lava

In a Mexican bullfighting arena, the bull chases a bull fighter (stock footage from "Bully for Bugs," 1953). Later, while everyone takes a siesta, the mice stage their own bull fight, Speedy Gonzales versus Sylvester, acting like a bull. Speedy uses hat pins, anvils, dynamite sticks, and glue to thwart "el gato". Sylvester fights back with rocket propelled jetskates which drill him into the ground, then blast him out of the arena!

CHILI WEATHER

Speedy Gonzales, Sylvester; Aug. 17; MM; Directed by Friz Freleng; Story by John Dunn; Animation by Gerry Chiniquy, Virgil Ross, Bob Matz, Lee Halpern, and Art Leonardi; Layouts by Hawley Pratt; Backgrounds by Tom O'Loughlin; Film Editor: Lee Gunther. Voice Characterization by Mel Blanc; Music by Bill Lava

In an attempt to get cheese from a food plant, Speedy leads Sylvester on a chase through the factory, onto the conveyer belts. Speedy narrowly misses being chopped, but Sylvester doesn't.

Speedy puts grease on the floor, causing the cat to slide into a vat of hot Tabasco sauce. Sylvester grabs Speedy on the bottle conveyer, but gets "bottle-capped." Sylvester chases Speedy, blinded by the bottlecap, running into a dehydrator and shrinks! Sylvester sees Speedy, thinks he's a giant mouse (At last! A real giant mouse!), and runs off.

CLAWS IN THE LEASE

Sylvester; Nov. 9; MM; Directed by Robert McKimson; Story by John Dunn; Animation by Warren Batchelder, George Grandpre, and Ted Bonnicksen; Layouts by Robert Gribbroek; Backgrounds by Richard H. Thomas; Film Editor: Treg Brown; Voice Characterization by Mel Blanc, Nancy Wible. Music by Bill Lava

After Junior is adopted by a old woman, Sylvester tries to get in as well. When the lady sees Sylvester drinking the milk, she hits him with her broom, and takes Junior in. Sylvester sneaks in the house and takes a can of cat food. In sneaking out, he passes the TV as the lady is turning it on. Appearing on the screen, Sylvester imitates a commercial for "Pussykins Cat Food." She gets wise and throws him after getting chucked one more time, Sylvester comes up with a plan to fill her house with mice, and then rescue her. Instead, the mice throw him, Junior, and the lady all out of the house, back into the dump.

1964

A MESSAGE TO GRACIAS

Speedy Gonzales, Sylvester; Feb. 8; LT; Directed by Robert McKimson; Story by John Dunn; Animation by George Grandpre, Ted Bonnicksen, and Warren Batchelder; Layouts and Backgrounds by Robert Gribbroek; Effects Animation by Harry Love; Film Editor: Treg Brown; Voice Characterization by Mel Blanc, Roger Green; Music by Bill Lava

Speedy is chosen by the General to deliver a message past Sylvester. Speedy runs over Sylvester and zooms off. Sylvester follows the mouse in a drag racer. When Speedy stops for lunch, the cat puts on the brakes, but crashes. Sylvester tries a rope trap, which only catches a wild beast. Sylvester also tries a motor boat and a lasso, but to no avail. Speedy delivers the message—"Happy Birthday." Speedy is upset that he went through all that trouble for such a trivial message and sets Sylvester loose on the mice. Fade out as cat chases the General into the distance.

FREUDY CAT

Sylvester, Hippety Hopper; Mar 14; LT; Directed by Robert McKimson; Story by Tedd Pierce; Animation by Ted Bonnicksen, Warren Batchelder, and George Grandpre; Layouts and Backgrounds by Robert Gribbroek; Film Editor: Treg Brown; Voice Characterization by Mel Blanc; Musical Direction by Robert McKimson

A cheater cartoon mainly comprised of footage from earlier Sylvester/Hippety Hopper epics. Sylvester runs home sweating and screaming, "Save me! Save me from the giant mouse!" Junior takes his father to Dr. Freud E. Katt, cat psychiatrist. Junior explains to the doctor, in flashback via scenes from "The Slap Hoppy Mouse" (1950) and "Cats A-Weigh" (1953). In the end, Hippety jumps into the doctor's office, and all three cats hop out!

NUTS AND VOLTS

Speedy Gonzales, Sylvester; Apr 25; LT; Directed by Friz Freleng; Story by John Dunn; Animation by Gerry Chiniquy, Virgil Ross, Bob Matz, Art Leonardi, and Lee Halpern; Layouts by Hawley Pratt; Backgrounds by Tom O'Loughlin; Film Editor: Treg Brown; Voice Characterization by Mel Blanc; Musical Direction by Bill Lava

Tired from all the chasing of Speedy, Sylvester decides to try to tackle the rodent with a series of electronic gadgets. First he sets up an electronic-eye beam outside his mouse hole that backfires, smashing him against the wall. Sylvester next tries a robot to chase the mouse but when Speedy shouts "Yee-Hah!" the robot jumps and smashes against the ceiling, eventually blasting itself and Sylvester. The cat rebuilds the machine and uses its extended arm to place a stick of dynamite into Speedy's hole. Speedy quickly places the dynamite behind Sylvester's back. Speedy gets into the technology, sending a robot dog after the lisping cat.

Claws in the Lease

A Message to Gracias

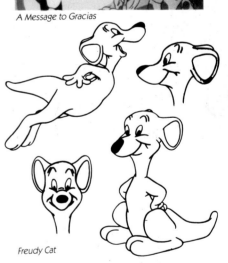
Freudy Cat

Nuts and Volts

151

HAWAIIAN AYE AYE

Tweety, Sylvester; June 27; MM; Directed by Gerry Chiniquy; Story by Tedd Pierce and Bill Daunch; Animation by Virgil Ross, Bob Matz, Art Leonardi, and Lee Halpern; Layouts by Robert Gribbroek; Backgrounds by Tom O'Loughlin; Film Editor: Treg Brown; Voice Characterization by Mel Blanc, June Foray; Musical Direction by Bill Lava

On her Hawaiian vacation, Granny goes to a luau, leaving Tweety alone with "Sharkey" the pet shark (who lives in a dog house in the ocean), as protection. Meanwhile, Sylvester spots Tweety and rows toward the island. Tweety sends Sharkey to "sic 'em." The fish bites into Sylvester's rubber raft, inflating Sharkey and sinking the cat. Sylvester tries a wire-and-pulley lift to get himself over to the island while dreaming of his delicious "broiled squab" meal. He fails to notice that he's heading into Sharkey's house! Other tactics: Sylvester tries a rubber underwater suit, but Sharkey cuts his air line; wooden stilts which are cut by legion of sawfish. When Granny and Tweety say "Aloha" to the islands, Sylvester is seen rowing after them, with Sharkey following.

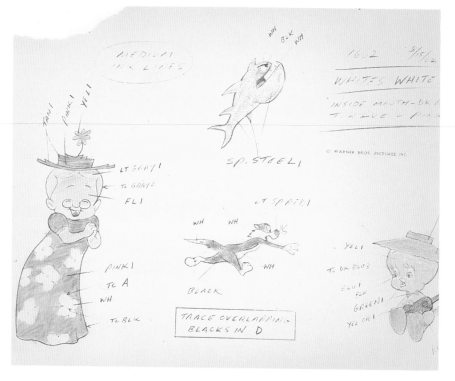

ROAD TO ANDALY

Speedy Gonzales, Sylvester; Dec 26; MM; directed by Friz Freleng; Co-Directed by Hawley Pratt; Story by John Dunn; Animation by Norm McCabe, Don Williams, and Bob Matz; Assistant Layout: Homer Jones; Backgrounds by Tom O'Loughlin; Film Editor: Lee Gunther; Voice Characterization by Mel Blanc; Musical Direction by Bill Lava

Sylvester employs Malcolm Falcon to help catch Speedy. Malcom goes after Speedy again, with Sylvester in tow, flying high into the sky. Sylvester yells "Let Go," and the cat goes crashing back to earth! Malcolm gets sucked into a jet engine, but returns to help Sylvester. Best bit: Malcolm brings Sylvester a lit dynamite from Speedy. Speedy restrains Malcolm by putting salt on the falcon's tail, but when Sylvester puts salt on his own tail to prove nothing happens, his tail falls off. Malcolm and Sylvester walk back to town to get some glue. Salt accidentally falls on Speedy's tail and he joins them on their trip into town.

1965

IT'S NICE TO HAVE A MOUSE AROUND THE HOUSE

Daffy Duck, Speedy Gonzales, Sylvester; Jan 16; LT; Directed by Friz Freleng; Co-Directed by Hawley Pratt; Story by John Dunn; Animation by Don Williams, Bob Matz, and Norm McCabe; Layouts by Dick Ung; Backgrounds by Tom O'Loughlin; Film Editor: Lee Gunther; Voice Characterization by Mel Blanc, and George Pearson; Musical Direction by Bill Lava

When Daffy Duck is brought in to help Sylvester catch Speedy, Speedy's trademark "Yee-Hah!" has Daffy jumping to the ceiling. Daffy sets a cheese trap, and nets Speedy but the mouse proceeds to drag the net and Daffy all over the house. Daffy tries glue outside his mouse hole, but another "Yee-Hah!" sends Daffy sticking to the ceiling! Daffy next tries a vacuum cleaner, but somehow winds up on the cement bottom of an empty pool. He then tries a robot mouse disposal, which ends up chasing Daffy through the neighborhood!

CATS AND BRUISES

Sylvester, Speedy Gonzales; Jan 30; MM; Directed by Friz Freleng; Co-Directed by Hawley Pratt; Story by John Dunn; Animation by Bob Matz, Norm McCabe, Don Williams, Manny Perez, Warren Batchelder, and Lee Halpern; Layouts by Dick Ung; Backgrounds by Tom O'Loughlin; Film Editor: Lee Gunther; Voice Characterization by Mel Blanc; Musical Direction by Bill Lava.

In a plot to ambush the mice fiesta, Sylvester dons a pair of "Mickey Mouse" ears and joins them in dance. The mice immediately get wise and run, leaving Speedy behind to heckle the "pussy-gato." Speedy leads Sylvester to a dog pound where his "Yee-Hah!" propels the cat into a snag of hungry dogs. Sylvester puts a rocket engine in his hot rod and chases Speedy. When the mouse stops, the cat forgets where the brakes are and crashes into the lake. Sylvester tries darts, boulders, rubber rafts, steel pipes, etc. to no avail.

It's Nice to Have a Mouse Around the House

THE WILD CHASE

The Road Runner, Speedy Gonzales, Sylvester; Feb 27; MM; Directed by Friz Freleng; Co-Directed by Hawley Pratt; Animation by Norman McCabe, Don Williams, Manny Perez, Warren Batchelder, and Laverne Harding; Layouts by Dick Ung; Backgrounds by Tom O'Loughlin; Film Editor: Lee Gunther; Voice Characterization by Mel Blanc; Musical Direction by Bill Lava.

This is essentially a Road Runner cartoon, re-using animation from earlier Chuck Jones films, with Speedy Gonzales and Sylvester drawn in as extras. Speedy and the Road Runner are racing. Meanwhile, the Coyote and Sylvester wait in the rocks with fork and knife. The cat and coyote try to propel boulders with a lever; with iron pellets in bird seed and cheese; and by dropping a huge flat rock off a mountain ledge. The two adversaries chase the speedy pair in a rocket car, which goes so fast they pass the mouse and bird and win the race!

Cats and Bruises

The Wild Chase

TWEETY'S CAMEO APPEARANCES
My Dream Is Yours (1949) feature film
"No Barking" (1954) Frisky Puppy/Claude Cat cartoon directed by Chuck Jones

SYLVESTER'S CAMEO APPEARANCE
"A TASTE OF CATNIP" (1966) Daffy Duck/Speedy Gonzales cartoon

FEATURE FILMS
Tweety and Sylvester appear in these feature films in both new animation and classic shorts"
Friz Freleng's Looney, Looney, Looney Bugs Bunny Movie (1981)
Bugs Bunny's 3rd Move: 1001 Rabbit Tales (1982)
Daffy Duck's Movie: Fantastic Island (1983)
Daffy Duck's Quackbusters (1988)

Below: Tweety appeared in a cameo in Chuck Jones' "No Barking." *Opposite:* Tweety and Sylvester in new footage from the 1989 television special "Bugs Bunny's Wild World of Sports"

TELEVISION

Tweety and Sylvester were featured in their classic cartoons on *The Bugs Bunny Show* (ABC, 1960-1962). Sylvester hosted the program, in new footage, six times, three with Tweety and three with his son Sylvester, Jr.

TELEVISION SPECIALS

"Bugs Bunny's Easter Special" (1977) contains "Birds Anonymous"
"A Connecticut Rabbit in King Arthur's Court" (1978) features Sylvester in a supporting role.
"Bugs Bunny's Howl-oween Special" (1978) contains "Scaredy Cat"
"Bugs Bunny's Thanksgiving Diet" (1979) contains scenes from "Trip for Tat"
"Bugs Bunny's Looney Christmas Tales" (1979) contains the new short "Bugs Bunny's Christmas Carol" which features Sylvester as Yosemite Sam's cat and Tweety as Tiny Tim. "Daffy Duck's Easter Special" (1980) contains the new short "The Yolks on You" featuring Sylvester.
"The Buys Bunny Mystery Special" (1980) features "Catty Cornered"
"Bugs Bunny's Wild World of Sports" (1989) features Tweety and Sylvester in new footage.
"Bugs Bunny's Overtures to Disaster" (1991) features Sylvester in a cameo role.

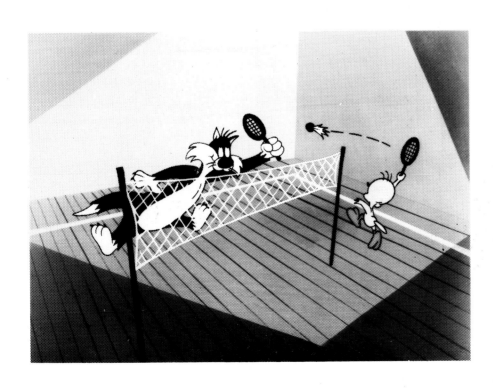

APPENDIX
This listing sorts all Sylvester and Tweety cartoons by directors, storymen, animators, layout artists and background artists

DIRECTORS
Gerry Chiniquy
1964 Hawaiian Aye Aye

Robert Clampett
1942 A Tale of Two Kitties
1944 Birdy and the Beast
1945 A Gruesome Twosome
1946 Kitty Cornered

Arthur Davis
1947 Doggone Cats
1947 Catch As Cats Can

Friz Freleng
1945 Life Wih Feathers
1945 Peck Up Your Troubles
1947 Tweetie Pie
1948 Kit For Cat
1948 Back Alley Oproar
1948 I Taw a Putty Tat
1949 Mouse Mazurka
1949 Bad 'Ol Putty Tat
1950 Home Tweet Home
1950 All A-Bir-r-d
1950 Canary Row
1950 Stooge For a Mouse
1951 Canned Feud
1951 Puddy Tat Twouble
1951 Room & Bird
1951 Tweety's S.O.S.
1951 Tweet Tweet Tweety
1952 Gift Wrapped
1952 Little Red Rodent Hood
1952 Ain't She Tweet
1952 Bird In a Guilty Cage
1952 Tree for Two
1953 Snow Business
1953 A Mouse Divided
1953 Fowl Weather
1953 Tom Tom Tomcat
1953 A Streetcat Named Sylvester
1953 Catty Cornered
1954 Dog Pounded
1954 Dr. Jerkyl's Hyde
1954 Muzzle Tough
1954 Satan's Waitin'
1954 By Work Of Mouse
1955 Sandy Claws
1955 Tweety's Circus
1955 A Kiddie's Kitty
1955 Red Riding Hoodwinked
1955 Heir Conditioned
1955 Pappy's Puppy
1956 Tweet & Sour
1956 Tree Cornered Tweety
1956 Tugboat Granny
1956 Yankee Dood It
1957 Tweet Zoo
1957 Tweety & The Beanstalk
1957 Birds Anonymous
1957 Greedy For Tweety
1957 Gonzales Tamales
1958 A Pizza Tweety Pie
1958 A Bird In a Bonnet
1959 Trick Or Tweet
1959 Tweet & Lovely
1959 Here Today, Gone Tamale
1959 Tweet Dreams
1960 Goldimouse & The Three Cats
1960 Hyde & Tweet
1960 Mouse & Garden
1960 Trip For Tat
1961 D'Fightin' Ones
1961 Rebel Without Claws
1961 The Pied Piper Of Guadalupe
1961 The Last Hungry Cat
1962 Mexican Boarders
1962 The Jet Cage
1963 Mexican Cat Dance
1963 Chili Weather
1964 Nuts & Volts
1964 Road To Andalay
1965 Its Nice To Have a Mouse Around The House
1965 Cats & Bruises
1965 The Wild Chase
1979 Bugs Bunnys Christmas Carol
1980 The Yolk's On You

Charles M. Jones
1948 Scaredy Cat
1950 The Scarlet Pumpernickel
1954 Claws For Alarm
1955 Jumpin' Jupiter

Robert McKimson
1947 Crowing Pains
1948 Hop Look & Listen
1949 Hippety Hopper
1950 Pop 'Im Pop!
1952 Who's Kitten Who
1952 Hoppy Go Lucky
1953 Cat's Aweigh
1954 Bell Hoppy
1955 Lighthouse Mouse
1956 Too Hop To Handle
1956 The Unexpected Pest
1956 The Slap-Hoppy Mouse
1957 Mouse-Taken Identity
1959 Cat's Paw
1960 West Of The Pesos
1961 Canary Woe
1961 Hoppy Daze
1961 Birds Of a Father
1962 Fish & Slips
1963 Claws In The Lease
1964 A Message To Gracias
1964 Freudy Cat

STORYMEN
Dave Detiege
1961 Birds Of a Father
1961 The Last Hungry Cat
1962 Fish & Slips

John Dunn
1961 The Pied Piper Of Guadalupe
1961 The Last Hungry Cat
1962 Mexican Boarders
1963 Mexican Cat Dance
1963 Chili Weather
1963 Claws in The Lease
1964 A Message To Gracias
1964 Road to Andaly
1964 Nuts & Volts
1965 It's Nice To Have a Mouse Around The House
1965 Cats & Bruises

Warren Foster
1942 A Tale Of Two Kitties
1944 Birdy & The Beast
1945 A Gruesome Twosome
1947 Crowing Pains
1948 Hop Look & Listen
1949 Hippety Hopper
1950 Pop 'Im Pop!
1951 Canned Feud
1951 Puddy Tat Twouble
1951 Tweety's S.O.S.
1951 Tweet Tweet Tweety
1952 Gift Wrapped
1952 Little Red Rodent Hood
1952 Ain't She Tweet
1952 Bird In a Guilty Cage
1952 Tree For Two
1953 Snow Business
1953 A Mouse Divided
1953 Fowl Weather
1953 Tom Tom Tomcat
1953 A Streetcat Named Sylvester
1953 Catty Cornered
1954 Dog Pounded
1954 Dr. Jerkyl's Hyde
1954 Muzzle Tough
1954 Satan's Waitin'
1954 By Word Of Mouse
1955 A Kiddie's Kitty
1955 Sandy Claws
1955 Tweety's Circus
1955 Red Riding Hoodwinked
1955 Heir Conditioned
1955 Pappy's Puppy
1956 Too Hop To Handle

1956 Tweet & Sour
1956 Tree Cornered Tweety
1956 The Unexpected Pest
1956 Tugboat Granny
1956 Yankee Dood It
1957 Tweet Zoo
1957 Tweety & The Beanstalk
1957 Birds Anonymous
1957 Greedy For Tweety
1958 A Pizza Tweety Pie
1958 A Bird In a Bonnet
1959 Trick Or Tweet
1959 Tweet & Lovely
1959 Tweet Dreams

Michael Maltese
1945 Peck Up Your Troubles
1948 Kit For Cat
1948 Back Alley Oproar
1948 Scaredy Cat
1950 The Scarlet Pumpernickel
1954 No Barking
1954 Claws For Alarm
1955 Jumpin' Jupiter
1959 Here Today, Gone Tamale
1960 Goldimouse & The Three Cats
1960 Trip For Tat

Sid Marcus
1955 Lighthouse Mouse

Dave Monahan
1947 Catch as Cats Can

Michael O'Connor
1966 A Taste Of Catnip

Tedd Pierce
1945 Life With Feathers
1948 Kit For Cat
1948 I Taw a Putty Tat
1949 Mouse Mazurka
1949 Bad Ol' Putty Tat
1950 All A-Bir-r-d
1950 Canary Row
1950 Home Tweet Home
1951 Room & Bird
1952 Who's Kitten Who
1952 Hoppy Go Lucky
1953 Cat's Aweigh
1954 Bell Hoppy
1956 The Slap-Hoppy Mouse
1957 Mouse-taken Identity
1959 Cat's Paw
1960 West Of The Pesos
1961 Canary Woe
1961 Hoppy Daze
1964 Hawaiian Aye Aye
1964 Freudy Cat

Lloyd Turner
1947 Doggone Cats

ANIMATORS
Warren Batchelder
1959 Cat's Paw
1960 West Of The Pesos
1961 Birds Of a Father
1961 Canary Woe
1961 Hoppy Daze
1962 Fish & Slips
1963 Claws In The Lease
1964 A Message to Gracias
1964 Freudy Cat
1965 Cats & Bruises
1965 The Wild Chase
1966 A Taste Of Catnip

Ted Bonnicksen
1954 By Word Of Mouse
1955 Tweety's Circus
1955 Red Riding Hoodwinked
1955 A Kiddie's Kitty
1956 The Slap-Hoppy Mouse
1956 The Unexpected Pest
1957 Mouse-taken Identity
1959 Cat's Paw
1960 West Of The Pesos
1961 Birds Of a Father
1961 Canary Woe
1961 Hoppy Daze
1962 Fish & Slips
1963 Claws in The Lease
1964 A Message To Gracias
1964 Freudy Cat

Pete Burness
1949 Hippety Hopper

John Carey
1947 Crowing Pains
1949 Hippety Hopper
1951 Canned Feud

Ken Champin
1945 Peck Up Your Troubles
1948 Kit For Cat
1948 Back Alley Oproar
1948 I Taw a Putty Tat
1949 Mouse Mazurka
1949 Bad Ol' Putty Tat
1950 All A-Bir-r-d
1950 Canary Row
1950 Home Tweet Home
1950 Stooge For a Mouse
1951 Room & Bird
1951 Tweety's S.O.S.
1951 Canned Feud
1951 Puddy Tat Twouble
1951 Tweet Tweet Tweety
1952 Ain't She Tweet
1952 Gift Wrapped
1952 Little Red Rodent Hood
1952 Bird In a Guilty Cage
1952 Tree For Two
1953 Snow Business
1953 A Mouse Divided
1953 Fowl Weather
1953 Tom Tom Tomcat
1953 A Streetcat Named Sylvester
1953 Catty Cornered

1954 Dog Pounded
1954 Dr. Jerkyl's Hyde
1954 Muzzle Tough
1954 Satan's Waitin'

Gerry Chiniquy
1948 Kit For Cat
1948 Back Alley Oproar
1948 I Taw a Putty Tat
1949 Mouse Mazurka
1949 Bad Ol' Putty Tat
1950 All A-Bir-r-d
1950 Canary Row
1950 Home Tweet Home
1950 Stooge For a Mouse
1954 By Word of Mouse
1955 Tweety's Circus
1955 Red Riding Hoodwinked
1955 Heir Conditioned
1955 A Kiddie's Kitty
1955 Pappy's Puppy
1956 Yankee Dood It
1956 Tweet & Sour
1956 Cornered Tweety
1956 Tugboat Granny
1957 Gonzales' Tamales
1957 Tweet Zoo
1957 Tweety & The Beanstalk
1957 Birds Anonymous
1957 Greedy For Tweety
1958 A Pizza Tweety Pie
1958 A Bird In a Bonnet
1959 Here Today Gone Tamale
1959 Trick Or Tweet
1959 Tweet & Lovely
1959 Tweet Dreams
1960 Goldimouse & The Three Cats
1960 Hyde & Tweet
1960 Mouse & Garden
1960 Trip For Tat
1961 D'Fightin' Ones
1961 Rebel Without Claws
1961 The Pied Peper Of Guadalupe
1961 The Last Hungry Cat
1962 Mexican Boarders
1963 Mexican Cat Dance
1963 Chili Weather
1964 Nuts & Volts

Herman Cohen
1947 Catch As Cats Can
1952 Hoppy Go Lucky
1953 Cat's Aweigh
1954 Bell Hoppy
1955 Lighthouse Mouse

Keith Darling
1955 Jumpin' Jupiter
1956 Too Hop To Handle
1956 The Slap-Hoppy Mouse

1956 The Unexpected Pest

Basil Davidovich
1945 A Gruesome Twosome
1947 Doggone Cats
1947 Catch As Cats Can

Arthur Davis
1955 Heir Conditioned
1955 A Kiddie's Kitty
1956 Yankee Dood It
1956 Tweet & Sour
1956 Tree Cornered Tweety
1956 Tugboat Granny
1957 Gonzales Tamales
1957 Tweet Zoo
1957 Tweety & The Beanstalk
1957 Birds Anonymous
1957 Greedy For Tweety
1958 A Pizza Tweety Pie
1958 A Bird In a Bonnet
1959 Here Today, Gone Tamale
1959 Trick Or Tweet
1959 Tweet & Lovely
1959 Tweet Dreams
1960 Goldimouse & The Three Cats
1960 Hyde & Tweet
1960 Mouse & Garden
1960 Trip For Tat
1961 D'Fightin' Ones
1961 Rebel Without Claws

Phil de Lara
1949 Hippety Hopper
1950 Pop 'Im Pop!
1952 Who's Kitten Who
1952 Hoppy Go Lucky
1953 Cats' Aweigh
1954 Bell Hoppy
1955 Lighthouse Mouse

Russ Dyson
1956 The Slap-Hoppy Mouse
1956 The Unexpected Pest

I. Ellis
1947 Crowing Pains
1948 Hop Look & Listen

Manny Gould
1945 A Gruesome Twosome
1946 Kitty Cornered
1947 Crowing Pains
1948 Hop Look & Listen

George Grandpre
1956 The Slap-Hoppy

Mouse
1956 The Unexpected Pest
1957 Mouse-Taken Identity
1959 Cat's Paw
1960 West of The Pesos
1961 Birds Of a Father
1961 Canary Woe
1961 Hoppy Daze
1962 Fish & Slips
1963 Claws In The Lease
1964 A Message To Gracias
1964 Freudy Cat
1966 A Taste Of Catnip

Lee Halpern
1961 The Last Hungry Cat
1962 Mexican Boarders
1962 The Jet Cage
1963 Chili Weather
1963 Mexican Cat Dance
1964 Hawaiian Aye Aye
1964 Nuts & Volts
1965 Cats & Bruises

Laverne Harding
1965 The Wild Chase

Ken Harris
1948 Scaredy Cat
1950 The Scarlet Pumpernickel
1954 No Barking
1954 Claws For Alarm
1955 Jumpin' Jupiter

Emery Hawkins
1947 Doggone Cats
1950 All A-Bir-r-d
1950 Canary Row
1950 Stooge For a Mouse
1952 Who's Kitten Who

Art Leonardi
1961 The Last Hungry Cat
1962 Mexican Boarders
1962 The Jet Cage
1963 Chili Weather
1963 Mexican Cat Dance
1964 Hawaiian Aye Aye
1964 Nuts & Volts

Abe Levitow
1954 Claws For Alarm
1955 Jumpin' Jupiter

Harry Love
1951 Tweet Tweet Tweety

Bob Matz
1961 The Pied Piper Of Guadalupe
1961 The Last Hungry Cat
1962 Mexican Boarders
1962 The Jet Cage
1963 Mexican Cat Dance
1963 Chili Weather
1964 Hawaiian Aye Aye
1964 Nuts & Volts
1965 It's Nice To Have a Mouse Around The House
1965 Cats & Bruises
1966 A Taste Of Catnip

Norm McCabe
1964 Road to Andaly
1965 It's Nice To Have a Mouse Around The House
1965 Cats & Bruises
1965 The Wild Chase
1966 A Taste Of Catnip

Charles McKimson
1947 Crowing Pains
1948 Hop Look & Listen
1949 Hippety Hopper
1950 Pop 'Im Pop!
1952 Who's Kitten Who
1952 Hoppy Go Lucky
1953 Cat's Aweigh
1954 Bell Hoppy
1955 Lighthouse Mouse

Robert McKimson
1956 Too Hop To Handle

Tom McKimson
1944 Birdy & The Beast

C. Melendez
1946 Kitty Cornered
1947 Doggone Cats
1947 Catch As Cats Can
1950 Pop 'Im Pop!

Phil Monroe
1948 Scaredy Cat
1950 The Scarlet Pumpernickel

Manny Perez
1948 Kit For Cat
1948 Back Alley Oproar
1948 I Taw a Putty Tat
1949 Mouse Mazurka
1949 Bad Ol' Putty Tat
1950 Pop 'Im Pop!
1951 Room & Bird
1951 Tweety's S.O.S.
1951 Canned Feud
1951 Puddy Tat Twouble
1952 Ain't She Tweet
1952 Gift Wrapped
1952 Little Red Rodent Hood
1952 Bird In a Guilty Cage
1952 Tree For Two
1953 Snow Business
1953 A Mouse Divided
1953 Fowl Weather
1953 Tom Tom Tomcat
1953 A Streetcat Named Sylvester
1953 Catty Cornered
1954 Dog Pounded
1954 Dr. Jerkyl's Hyde
1954 Muzzle Tough
1954 Satan's Waitin'
1955 Sandy Claws
1965 Cats & Bruises
1965 The Wild Chase
1966 A Case Of Catnip

Tom Ray
1959 Cat's Paw
1960 West Of The Pesos
1960 Trip For Tat
1961 Canary Woe
1961 Hoppy Daze

Virgil Ross
1945 Life With Feathers
1948 Kit For Cat
1948 Back Alley Oproar
1948 I Taw a Putty Tat
1949 Mouse Mazurka
1949 Bad Ol 'Putty Tat
1950 All A-Bir-r-d
1950 Canary Row
1950 Home Tweet Home
1950 Stooge For a Mouse
1951 Room & Bird
1951 Tweety's S.O.S.
1951 Canned Feud
1951 Puddy Tat Twouble
1951 Tweet Tweet Tweety
1952 Ain't She Tweet
1952 Gift Wrapped
1952 Little Red Rodent Hood
1952 Bird In Guilty Cage
1952 Tree For Two
1953 Snow Business
1953 A Mouse Divided

1953 Fowl Weather
1953 Tom Tom Tomcat
1953 A Streetcat Named Sylvester
1953 Catty Cornered
1954 Dr. Jerkyl's Hyde
1954 Muzzle Tough
1954 Satan's Waitin'
1955 Sandy Claws
1955 Heir Conditioned
1956 Yankee Dood It
1956 Tweet & Sour
1956 Tree Cornered Tweety
1956 Tugboat Granny
1957 Gonzales Tamales
1957 Tweet Zoo
1957 Tweety & The Beanstalk
1957 Birds Anonymous
1957 Greedy For Tweety
1958 A Pizza Tweety Pie
1958 A Bird In a Bonnet
1959 Here Today, Gone Tamale
1959 Trick Or Tweet
1959 Tweet & Lovely
1959 Tweet Dreams
1960 Goldimouse & The Three Cats
1960 Hyde & Tweet
1960 Mouse & Garden
1960 Trip for Tat
1961 D'Fightin' Ones
1961 Rebel Without Claws
1961 The Pied Piper of Guadalupe
1961 The Last Hungry Cat
1962 Mexican Boarders
1962 The Jet Cage
1963 Mexican Cat Dance
1963 Chili Weather
1964 Hawaiian Aye Aye
1964 Nuts & Volts

Rod Scribner
1942 A Tale Of Two Kitties
1945 A Gruesome Twosome
1946 Kitty Cornered
1950 Pop 'em Pop!
1952 Who's Kitten Who
1952 Hoppy Go Luck
1953 Cat's Aweigh
1954 Bell Hoppy
1955 Lighthouse Mouse

Richard Thompson
1954 Claws For Alarm
1955 Jumpin' Jupiter

Lloyd Vaughan
1948 Scaredy Cat
1950 The Scarlet Pumpernickel
1954 Claws For Alarm

Ben Washam
1948 Scaredy Cat
1950 The Scaredy Pumpernickel
1954 Claws For Alarm
1954 By Word of Mouse

Don Williams
1947 Doggone Cats
1947 Catch As Cats Can
1964 Road To Andaly
1965 It's Nice To Have a Mouse Around The House
1965 Cats & Bruises
1965 The Wild Chase

LAYOUTS AND BACKGROUNDS
Dorcy Howard
1946 Kitty Kornered

Thomas McKimson
1945 A Gruesome Twosome
1946 Kitty Cornered

Michael Sasanoff
1945 A Gruesome Twosome

LAYOUTS
Robert Givens
1952 Hoppy Go Lucky
1953 Cat's Aweigh
1954 Bell Hoppy
1955 Lighthouse Mouse
1955 Jumpin' Jupiter
1960 West Of The Pesos

Robert Gribbroek
1948 Scaredy Cat
1950 The Scarlet Pumpernickel
1956 The Slap-Hoppy Mouse
1956 The Unexpected Pest
1957 Mouse-Taken Identity
1959 Cat's Paw
1961 Birds Of a Father
1961 Canary Woe
1961 Hoppy Daze
1962 Fish & Slips
1963 Claws In The Lease
1964 A Message To Gracias
1964 Hawaiian Aye Aye
1964 Freudy Cat

Homer Jones
1964 Road To Andaly

Maurice Noble
1954 Claws For Alarm
1954 No Barking

Hawley Pratt
1948 Kit for Cat
1948 Back Alley Oproar

1948 I Taw a Putty Tat
1949 Mouse Mazurka
1949 Bad Ol' Putty Tat
1950 All A-Bir-r-d
1950 Canary Row
1950 Home Tweet Home
1950 Stooge For a Mouse
1951 Room & Bird
1951 Tweety's S.O.S.
1951 Canned Feud
1951 Putty Tat Twouble
1951 Tweet Tweet Tweety
1952 Ain't She Tweet
1952 Gift Wrapped
1952 Little Red Rodent Hood
1952 Bird In a Guilty Cage
1952 Tree For Two
1953 Snow Business
1953 A Mouse Divided
1953 Fowl Weather
1953 Tom Tom Tomcat
1953 A Streetcat Named Sylvester
1953 Catty Cornered
1954 Dog Pounded
1954 Dr. Jerkyl's Hyde
1954 Muzzle Tough
1954 Satan's Waitin'
1954 By Word of Mouse
1955 Sandy Claws
1955 Tweety's Circus
1955 Red Riding Hoodwinked
1955 Heir Conditioned
1955 A Kiddie's Kitty
1955 Pappy's Puppy
1956 Yankee Dood It
1956 Tweet & Sour
1956 Tree Cornered Tweety
1956 Tugboat Granny
1957 Gonzales Tamales
1957 Tweet Zoo
1957 Tweety & The Beanstalk
1957 Birds Anonymous
1957 Greedy For Tweety
1958 A Pizza Tweety Pie
1958 A Bird In a Bonnet
1959 Here Today, Gone Tamale
1959 Trick or Tweet
1959 Tweet & Lovely
1960 Goldimouse & The Three Cats
1960 Hyde & Tweet
1960 Mouse & Garden
1960 Trip For Tat
1961 D' Fightin' Ones
1961 Rebel Without Claws
1962 The Jet Cage
1963 Mexican Cat Dance
1963 Chili Weather
1964 Nuts & Volts

Don Smith

1947 Catch As Cats Can
1947 Doggone Cats

Dick Ung

1965 It's Nice To Have a Mouse Around The House
1965 Cats & Bruises
1965 The Wild Chase
1966 A Taste Of Catnip

Cornett Wood

1947 Crowing Pains
1948 Hop Look & Listen
1949 Hippety Hopper
1950 Pop 'Im Pop

BACK-GROUNDS
Peter Alvarado

1948 Scaredy Cat
1950 The Scarlet Pumpernickel
1952 Who's Kitten Who

Bill Butler

1957 Mouse-Taken Identity
1959 Cat's Paw
1960 West Of The Pesos
1961 Birds Of a Father
1961 Canary Woe

Philip de Guard

1947 Catch As Cats Can
1947 Doggone Cats
1954 No Barking
1954 Claws For Alarm
1955 Jumpin' Jupiter

Boris Gorelick

1957 Gonzales Tamales
1957 Birds Anonymous
1957 Greedy For Tweety

Paul Julian

1948 Kit For Cat
1948 Back Alley Oproar
1948 I Taw a Putty Tat
1949 Mouse Mazurka
1949 Bad Ol' Putty Tat
1950 All A-Bir-r-d
1950 Canary Row
1950 Stooge For a Mouse
1951 Room & Bird
1951 Tweety's S.O.S.
1951 Canned Feud
1951 Putty Tat Twouble
1951 Tweet Tweet Tweety

Carlos Manriquez

1953 Snow Business

Tom O'Loughlin

1958 A Pizza Tweety
1958 A Bird In a Bonnet
1959 Here Today, Gone Tamale
1959 Trick Or Tweet
1959 Tweet & Lovely
1960 Goldimouse & The Three Cats

1960 Hyde & Tweet
1960 Mouse & Garden
1960 Trip For Tat
1961 D' Fightin' Ones
1961 Rebel Without Claws
1961 The Pied Piper Of Guadalupe
1961 The Last Hungry Cat
1962 Mexican Boarders
1962 The Jet Cage
1963 Mexican Cat Dance
1963 Chili Weather
1964 Hawaiian Aye Aye
1964 Road To Andaly
1964 Nuts & Volts
1965 It's Nice To Have a Mouse Around The House
1965 Cats & Bruises
1965 The Wild Chase
1966 A Taste Of Catnip

Bob Singer

1961 Hoppy Daze

Richard H Thomas

1947 Crowing Pains
1948 Hop Look & Listen
1949 Hippety Hopper
1950 Pop 'em Pop!
1952 Who's Kitten Who
1952 Hoppy Go Lucky
1953 Cat's Aweigh
1954 Bell Hoppy
1955 Lighthouse Mouse
1956 Too Hop To Handle Layouts & Backgrounds
1956 The Slap-Hoppy Mouse
1956 The Unexpected Pest
1963 Claws In The Lease

Irv Wyner

1952 Ain't She Tweet
1952 Gift Wrapped
1952 Little Red Rodent Hood
1952 Bird In a Guilty Cage
1952 Tree For Two
1953 A Mouse Divided
1953 Fowl Weather
1953 Tom Tom Tomcat
1953 A Streetcat Named Sylvester
1953 Catty Cornered
1954 Dog Pounded
1954 Dr. Jerkyl's Hide
1954 Muzzle Tough
1954 Satan's Waitin'
1954 By Word Of Mouse
1955 Sandy Claws
1955 Tweety's Circus
1955 Red Riding Hoodwinked
1955 Heir Conditioned

1955 A Kiddie's Kitty
1955 Pappy's Puppy
1956 Yankee Dood It
1956 Tweet & Sour
1956 Tree Cornered Tweety
1956 Tugboat Granny
1957 Tweet Zoo

Index of Cartoons
(Numbers in boldface refer to pictures)

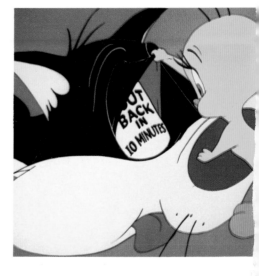